From Hive to Honey

Beekeeping for Beginners to Raising a Healthy Honeybee Colony and Producing Delicious Honey

Anthony Smalls

© **Copyright 2023 by Anthony Smalls (Independently published) - All rights reserved.**

The content contained within this book may not be reproduced, duplicated, or transmitted without direct written permission from the author or the publisher.

Under no circumstances will any blame or legal responsibility be held against the publisher, or author, for any damages, reparation, or monetary loss due to the information contained within this book, either directly or indirectly.

Legal Notice:

This book is copyright protected. It is only for personal use. You cannot amend, distribute, sell, use, quote, or paraphrase any part, or the content within this book, without the author's or publisher's consent.

Disclaimer Notice:

Please note that the information in this document is for educational and entertainment purposes only. All effort has been executed to present accurate, up-to-date, reliable, and complete information. No warranties of any kind are declared or implied. Readers acknowledge that the author is not engaging in the rendering of legal, financial, medical, or professional advice. The content within this book has been derived from various sources. Please consult a licensed professional before attempting any techniques outlined in this book.

By reading this document, the reader agrees that under no circumstances is the author responsible for any direct or indirect losses incurred due to the use of the information contained within this document, including, but not limited to, errors, omissions, or inaccuracies.

Contents

Introduction   1

1. Chapter 1: What Is Beekeeping?   3
   Beekeeping and Its Importance
   The History of Beekeeping
   The Evolution of Honey and Hives
   Roles Bees Play in Pollination
   Foods that Bees Can pollinate
   Other Bee Species Involved in Pollination
   Bees and the Environment
   Threats to the Bee Population
   Benefits of Beekeeping

2. Chapter 2: Bee Anatomy and Biology   18
   Body Parts
   The Lifecycle of Bees
   The Roles of Bees
   Maintaining the Hive

3. Chapter 3: Setting Up Your Apiary　　　　　31
    Apiaries: What You Should Know
    Factors to Consider Before Setting Up an Apiary
    Equipment Needed to Set Up an Apiary
    Getting Honey Bees for Your Apiary

4. Chapter 4: Hive Management and Honey　　42
   Production
    The Importance of Hive Management
    Best Management Practices
    Maximizing Honey Production

5. Chapter 5: Beekeeping Safety and Disease　　55
   Management
    Safety Gear
    Hive-Handling Techniques
    Common Diseases That Affect Bees

6. Chapter 6: Harvesting Honey　　　　　　　68
    When to Harvest Honey
    How to Harvest Your Honey
    How to Safely Store Honey
    Storing Honey for Personal Use
    Storing Honey for Long Term

7. Chapter 7: Beyond Honey: Other Bee Products　　78

Beeswax

   Potential Health Benefits

   Bee Pollen

   Skin Health

   Bee Venom

8. Chapter 8: Beekeeping for a Sustainable Future   88

   The Importance of Environmentally Friendly Beekeeping Practices

   Advocating for the Protection of Bees for a Sustainable Future

Conclusion   100

References   102

Introduction

Dive into the captivating world of beekeeping, where you'll feel connected with nature and get the chance to reap its sweet rewards. Whether you are fascinated by these amazing creatures and want to study them or dream of harvesting pure honey all by yourself, this book will be an excellent companion in your beekeeping journey.

Keeping aspiring beekeepers in mind, this comprehensive guide will improve the knowledge and skills you need to maintain honeybee colonies. Unlike other beekeeping books, this one provides a beginner-friendly approach that fosters your understanding of beekeeping and discovering the actual benefits, all while you gain confidence and the required knowledge to become a skilled beekeeper.

If you are new to beekeeping and want to master it, this book will take you through everything you need. It will keep it simple to understand so readers from all backgrounds can learn.

Instructions and relevant information are presented in an organized manner to take you through the whole beekeeping process. Information like care tips, preventing common issues, choosing the right equipment, and harvesting techniques are all covered here.

It also includes fascinating information regarding the intricate dynamics of honeybee colonies, the different roles these bees carry out to maintain their ecosystem, and their life cycle. Although bees have a sophisticated life cycle and other responsibilities, they play a crucial role in pollination.

You'll find valuable insights on common diseases, pest control tips, practical techniques to manage these issues, and the best methods to maintain the health of your bees for a thriving honeybee colony.

Armed with all this knowledge, you'll be able to ensure the health and well-being of your honeybee colony and produce pure, delicious honey in no time.

Chapter One

Chapter 1: What Is Beekeeping?

Since bees hold such immense power over the ecosystem, it is no surprise that humans find themselves so drawn to them. Their pollination function is crucial in maintaining environmental well-being. Beekeeping has been around since ancient times and allows enthusiasts to explore this magnificent world further by giving insight into how bees coexist so seamlessly in their surroundings. Bee cultivation or beekeeping represents a process that allows individuals to care for these essential insects and aims to maintain their hives while extracting things like honey or wax.

In this chapter aimed at newcomers, you will find an in-depth introduction to its intricacies, history, and evolution. The significant role played by these insect pollinators and their impacts on maintaining environmental habitats will be detailed, along with evidence supporting their beneficial effects on the ecosystem. In the later part of this chapter, you will learn why these efforts are worthwhile for both the short and long term.

Beekeeping and Its Importance

Beekeeping or apiculture is the careful management of domesticated colonies of honeybees (Apis genus) that typically reside within indoor artificial structures called beehives. Other species beyond honeybees, like Melipona stingless bees, may also be used for honey-production-based businesses or cultural practices.

Apiarists, also known as beekeepers, diligently look after bee colonies, collecting honeycomb products like wax pellets or nutrient-rich substances like royal jelly besides the targeted collection of raw liquid honey. Sometimes, they make additional profit from farming out "pollination services" on farms besides rearing queen bees. These are all very lucrative income streams derived from this process-oriented industry.

The History of Beekeeping

Evidence of the evolution of humans as collectors seeking nature's bounty, known as wild honey, originated in Spain some 15000 years ago. Spanish people harvested their first golden drops by creating makeshift hives, which served up prime opportunities to exploit this sweet treat without fully understanding bees or anything about them.

Over ten millennia later, humans found recorded proof made around 4000 BCE highlighting advancements in beekeeping techniques from much further East, within ancient Egypt's borders. Beekeepers around that time rode traffic waves up and down the Nile River following pleasant weather temperatures and blooming flowers.

Ancient Egyptians placed honey in their burial offerings as a luxury item to ensure a happy afterlife. Archeologists found sealed jars containing well-preserved samples of this ancient honey.

Early civilizations learned how to effectively harvest high-quality honey without causing harm. They used smoke from torches on bees, allowing them to collect honey easily. But it was not exactly perfect, and entire bee colonies died for the sake of acquiring just one jar of honey. Colonies were killed by burning sulfur once it was time for extraction. That prevented individual bees from escaping suffocation leading up to a distinct loss.

The Evolution of Honey and Hives

Humans have used honey for thousands of years, dating to around 2100 BC. Its consumption gave people an appreciation for the hardworking bees that produced it and highlighted the risks beekeepers took to harvest it. Primitive communities likely valued honey as a welcome addition to their simple diets, which made finding a wild hive all the more exciting and its location a closely guarded secret. Beyond its taste, honey's health benefits make it a desirable and valuable treat.

The Egyptians are considered the first beekeepers in history as they attempted to domesticate bees and created "natural" hives from hollow trees and logs that mimicked their natural habitat. They developed beekeeping techniques and moved their hives according to weather and flowering patterns.

At that time, honey was considered a luxury reserved only for high society. The ancient Egyptians even buried jars of honey with royal treasures, some of which were found intact and well-preserved.

Beekeeping continued to spread throughout Europe, Greece, and Rome, where Virgil, the famous Roman poet, wrote guides on beekeeping techniques. Spanish conquerors also took beehives with them during their conquests in South America.

In the 17th Century, George Wheler documented his travels through Greece, where he observed Greeks keeping beehives with removable frames that allowed for easier extraction of honey – an innovation in beekeeping technology at the time.

Although some beekeepers prefer to build their hives in trees, wild hives clinging onto cliffs offer greater security because they discourage hunters. Nevertheless, some determined individuals find ways of working together and using ropes when necessary to ascend or descend dangerous canyons and retrieve the honey.

In 1770, Thomas Wildman wrote "A Treatise on the Management of Bees," offering practical guidelines for constructing beehives that prioritized the well-being of bees during the management process. To this day, his innovative ways remain popular.

He used a removable woven lid placed atop an open-topped skep along with hanging frames that provide structure for bee-made honeycombs. The stacked skep aspect gives migrating bees another home once they have filled up one hive, which minimizes potential damage from harvesting previously occupied skeps.

Lorenzo Lorraine Langstroth is known as the innovator who transformed American Beekeeping in 1851. His contributions are highly regarded, with one notable breakthrough being the "bee space" concept that builds upon Thomas Wildman's original idea. This method involved creating a narrow gap of one centimeter between frames to prevent bees from forming tiny comb or propolis bridges between structures. Thanks to this approach, beekeepers can now seamlessly manage hives by safely removing frames without causing damage to sections developed by bees and maintaining their health and comfort. In addition, Langstroth elevated hive designs by introducing sturdy wooden boxes as an alternative to woven skeps.

Roles Bees Play in Pollination

The mid-1700s saw the recognition of bees as experts and indispensable pollinators. However, it was not until around 1750 that their importance was officially recorded. In modern times, beekeeping practices have evolved to utilize hives for crop pollination rather than focusing solely on honey production. Danish farmers adopted this method during the 1930s by renting hives from local beekeepers for improved crop growth; today, this strategy is widely used and heavily prevalent in California, where proper cross-fertilization measures are crucial to almond tree production facilitated by effective integration with agricultural beekeeping approach. These benefits also extend to the neighborhood level, with some attributing their fruitful harvests to the bee-rearing activities of neighbors.

Pollination by bees is crucial for plant reproduction since many plants rely on bees or other insects. This process begins when a bee collects nectar and pollen from a flower; as they gather these materials, some of the male reproductive organs' pollen sticks to their body hairs.

Soon after, when the bee visits another flower, this same pollen comes into contact with the female reproductive organ, resulting in fertilization, eventually leading to fruit development. Over time, plants have evolved ways of attracting more bees (and other pollinators) to reproduce more successfully. These attractive features include open flowering or tubular varieties that yield lots of nectar and pollen, while brightly colored petals or sweet fragrances make them all the more enticing. Bee pollination has also been found beneficial for fruit production because trees that receive multiple visits tend to produce larger-sized fruits with greater consistency than those visited less often.

Foods that Bees Can pollinate

Bees are crucial in pollinating many food sources, from fruits to vegetables to nuts and grains. With so much at stake in food security, it is worth appreciating the work they do every day.

Here's an overview of some foods that rely heavily on bee pollination for optimal growth: alfalfa, almonds, asparagus, beans, apples, blackberries, blueberries, beets, sprouts, buckwheat, brussels, cabbage, cantaloupe, cauliflower, cherries chestnuts, celery, chives, cranberries, cucumbers, clover, currants, flax, garlic, eggplant, gooseberries, grapes, kale, lettuce, horseradish, mustard, onions, peaches, pears, parsley, plums, pumpkins, raspberries, rhubarb, radishes, squash, sunflowers, sweet potatoes strawberries, and turnip watermelon.

Other Bee Species Involved in Pollination

Although honeybees receive much attention for being prolific pollinators, it must be remembered that there are other bee species whose contribution towards crop production and environmental balance should be appreciated. Learning about these varieties offers an opportunity to understand the diversity within the typically overlooked ecosystem of these creatures.

Bumblebees stand out as formidable pollinators distinguished by their buzz (sonication) pollination techniques during flower interaction that enable them to extract pollen from tight holding mechanisms and then deliver it upon contact with other flowers producing significant fruit yield benefits like blueberries or cranberries alongside tomato cultivation.

Mason bees deserve recognition, too, because they display exceptional artisan skills in nest-building through unique methods that involve constructing homes from either mud or chewed leaves as required. This earned them the nickname "mason" bee and became an indispensable asset for successful fruit tree orchard pollination in apple, peach, and almond cultivation.

Carpenter bees impress with distinctive deep flower pollination abilities. They are experts at using robust jaws for retrieving nectar effectively from long corolla flowers leading to valuable reproductive success chances, which had been previously problematic in other species of bees.

The sight of leafcutter bees skillfully slicing round pieces off leaves to build their nests fascinates anyone who comes across it. Moreover, these outstanding insects showcase remarkable abilities when gathering pollen from the bottoms of their abdomen, especially since they ensure that alfalfa crops are adequately pollinated, leading to tremendous implications for agriculture. It's safe to say that these tiny creatures have a monumental impact!

While mining or digger-bees might not catch the limelight like some other bee species, there is no denying how vital their role is. For instance, they pollinate wildflowers and dandelions in early spring, benefiting woodland and meadow ecosystems.

Bees and the Environment

Over millions of years, bees have formed a mutually beneficial partnership with flowering plants by evolving together through effective pollination and foraging behaviors. Plants are essential food providers (nectar and pollen) for bees' well-being. In contrast, bees facilitate plant fertilization by spreading pollen from the plant's male parts to female parts resulting in seed and fruit production and thereby benefiting wildlife that depends on them.

Moreover, their ability to identify alterations in habitat quality and exposure to pesticides and climate change makes them essential for determining ecological health. Any shifts in bee populations serve as environmental indicators cautioning against possible harmful effects for other species and ecosystems.

Threats to the Bee Population

There is a growing concern over the decline of bee populations across the globe in recent years due to multiple threats they face in the changing world environment. One significant challenge comes from agricultural practices that rely heavily on pesticides, specifically widely used neonicotinoids which contribute to adverse health outcomes like behavioral changes, reproductive issues, and the decline in the health of pollinators.

Also, it's hard for bees not to be accidentally exposed to contamination during foraging activities leading to poisoning and further endangering their species' survival. Climate change, like reduced temperatures and precipitation patterns, poses additional risks by disrupting the environmental conditions these insects need to thrive. This causes a mismatch between flowering plants and active bees, making pollen access difficult and ultimately reducing reproductive success.

Furthermore, invasive species like Varroa mites play a significant role in diminishing bee populations. Due to their ability to target weaker bees, they can weaken the hive's overall immunity system making bees vulnerable to infections and diseases that could threaten their entire colony's survival. Caring for these critical insects will require addressing these key challenges effectively.

Benefits of Beekeeping

Anyone Can Be a Beekeeper

Some years ago, this hobby was initially daunting because self-sufficiency required carpentry skill mastery which was difficult for many people interested in taking up beekeeping. But these days, with complete pre-made kits widely available and equipment vendors who can supply on demand, novice beekeepers can now commit to enjoying the process without experiencing these additional challenges.

Individuals living in urban settings or areas with limited space need not feel limited as well. Adaptations can always be made to create the perfect setup regardless of where you live.

Accessibility is not an issue either, as specially designed equipment and hives catering towards mobility needs or ability levels may require assistance for all interested parties.

As a bonus, nothing beats being part of a supportive, like-minded community! You'll get to share tips and tricks while gaining access to an array of readily available resources for making a success out of this hobby — making it even more enjoyable.

It Provides General Gardening Knowledge

The value of apiculture is not limited to honey production. It extends well beyond local agriculture as well. Bees play an essential role in helping farmers and communities make proper decisions on suitable crop planting methods through their unique challenges, which are easy for beekeepers to observe and by directly using the right tools like hive adjustments tailored for each season's weather changes!

The practical knowledge gained from this process includes understanding critical aspects of pollination techniques like recognizing harmful pests affecting agricultural yields or mastering efficient pesticide uses that contribute towards maintaining a safe environment conducive to the healthy growth of plants. Overall, participation in these activities empowers people with immense knowledge about the natural world around them.

You Get to Join Beekeeping Community

When embarking on your journey as a beekeeper, you can gain valuable knowledge from fellow enthusiasts who share your passion for bees. Fortunately, the beekeeping community is rich with expertise and insight to tap into as you learn about caring for honeybees. To connect with this community, consider reaching out through social media or seeking out nearby beekeeping clubs or associations. Additionally, don't hesitate to ask local beekeepers if they might be willing to mentor and guide you in the early stages of your new hobby.

Many of these organizations offer resources that can be especially helpful to beginners. For instance, some provide loaner honey extractors and other equipment to members just starting. It's worth exploring the options in your area to take advantage of these opportunities!

Honeybees play an essential role as pollinators, but unfortunately, their populations have been threatened in recent years. By becoming a beekeeper, you can ensure these vital creatures thrive for future generations. You can also use your position within the beekeeping community to spread awareness about pollinator health and inspire others to take up this rewarding hobby.

Urban Beekeeping Benefits the Ecosystem

Urban beekeeping has become quite popular in recent years as people increasingly embrace this practice beyond traditional rural settings. Through urban beekeeping efforts, beekeepers have established residential and city-area beehives where housing honeybees seemed impossible before.

When working with bees, safety is paramount—both from a human perspective and also considering how best to ensure these newest urban residents thrive well amidst all activities distinctly present within cities.

The biodiversity of flowers found within cities leads to superior yields regarding honey bee productivity relative to rural areas, thereby making it enjoyable because it allows you to escape from bustling city life—unleashing some serenity at last.

Rooftops make housing colonies easier through various means available to ease clustering. That provides an optimal setup for urban beekeeping endeavors to thrive.

Communities also benefit from urban beekeeping since plant ecosystems like community gardens, parks, and the general environment get pollinated and promoted regarding fruiting and seed production. This yields widespread benefits of food security, ecological health, and the overall environmental appeal to city inhabitants.

Beeswax and Other Products

Although frequently overshadowed in popularity by honey, you should not discount the versatility of beeswax as a worthy beneficial product from beekeeping activities. This is a component naturally used by young worker bees when building honeycombs within hives; once processed via melting and filtering methods, beeswax has countless possibilities for creating all-natural products for practical household use or heartfelt gifting.

Utilizing its benefits, you can produce personal skincare pieces like lip balm, lotion, and soap while creating eco-friendly items like wax food wraps or chemical-free wood furniture polish and cutting board conditioner. If you'd prefer a more artistic pursuit with this resourceful material, try crafting unique candle designs that range from simple taper or votive styles to stunning carvings. Additionally, thanks to antimicrobial compounds that soothe skin concerns, it's easy to see why beauty industry experts specifically include beeswax in formulas intended for sensitive skin.

You Get Access to the Purest Form of Honey

One of the great things about being a beekeeper is having easy access to honey. You have to be patient in any case. Maintaining these busy critters takes time, devotion, and tact. That being said, your effort will be rewarded handsomely once you have access to fresh and raw honey year-round; however, you wish to consume it.

Apart from enjoying fresh honey, there is a growing demand for beeswax and honey products from local communities. Delight existing or new customers at local events using quality bottles or cut comb containers that safeguard your product during transport; you can even add custom labels to attract more customers.

You Will Learn Everyday

Bee colonies offer endless opportunities for gaining new knowledge. Unique subjects like comb-cell stacking structures or colony organization allow keepers never to stop learning about these little creatures' remarkable work and how they maintain communication patterns among themselves.

Whether you visit your hives daily or less frequently, observing them at work will teach you so much about teamwork, social hierarchy, and specialization of tasks. Participating in virtual or in-person classes, books, and other resources can further expand your knowledge.

You've gained a comprehensive understanding of the symbiotic relationships between bees and nature itself. This mutually beneficial relationship leads humans to exciting realizations about the possible positive impact beekeeping can have on the environment. Not only is it a total package solution for restoring habitats, promoting biodiversity, and natural pest control farming methods when carried out sustainably, but beekeeping also has significant well-being benefits for beekeepers.

Chapter Two

Chapter 2: Bee Anatomy and Biology

Bees are undoubtedly fascinating creatures famous for their complex social living and their vital role in making flora and fauna bloom through pollination. The remarkable body structure and unique characteristics make these buzzing insects an essential ecosystem component. In this chapter, you'll learn about their anatomy, the different roles these bees play in a beehive, and some practical strategies you can use to maintain the beehive while keeping them safe, healthy, and thriving.

Body Parts

Exoskeleton

Like other insects, bees have an exoskeleton, a rigid external covering that protects and supports their bodies. Made of chitin, the exoskeleton also helps prevent water loss and provides a surface for muscle attachment.

Head

The head of a bee contains several important structures. The most prominent are the compound eyes, which enable them to see ultraviolet light and distinguish colors. Bees also have three simple eyes, known as ocelli, which aid navigation and orientation. The head also has antennae that help bees sense odors and vibrations in the environment.

Antennae

Bees have a pair of highly sensitive antennae on the head that can detect a range of environmental variables. These include temperature, humidity, carbon dioxide levels, wind speed, weak electric fields, and gravity. They also contain receptors for smell, touch, and taste. These are used to communicate with the colony, navigate, and locate food sources.

Eyes

Bees have compound eyes located on either side of their heads. Their eyes are made of numerous ommatidia (individual lenses), which give them crystal-clear vision.

Mouthparts

Bees possess specialized mouthparts designed for various functions. The most notable are the mandibles, which allow them to manipulate and chew materials like wax and resin. Bees also have a long, tube-like proboscis called a tongue or a glossa, used for sipping nectar from flowers.

Mandibles

The mandibles or the bee's jaws are well-adapted to chewing and nibbling on food. Besides making food easier to consume, they use them to transfer pollen, build their hives, and craft wax. The jaws are also strong enough to let the bees defend themselves.

Thorax

It's the middle section of the bee's body and has legs, wings and encloses several vital internal structures.

Wings

Bees have two pairs of wings: forewings and hindwings. They are transparent and membranous, allowing the bees to fly and maneuver freely, making easy aerial movements. The rapid beating movement of the wings creates enough air resistance and lift to let the bees carry themselves through the air at a fast pace. This rapid movement also makes it easier for the bees to hover over flowers and other nectar sources while maintaining control in mid-air.

Legs

Their six legs are of different lengths and are used for various tasks. Specialized structures like pads, claws, and hair are present on the legs to let the bees carry out their everyday routine. Commonly, they use their legs to walk while gripping surfaces, collecting pollen, communicating, and grooming their bodies.

Abdomen

It houses several organs and specialized structures.

Stinger

Female bees, like worker bees and queens, possess a modified ovipositor known as a stinger. It is located at the end of their abdomen. They primarily use their stinger as a defensive weapon, injecting venom into predators or animals they perceive as threats. However, when a bee stings, the stinger gets lodged in the skin as the venom is injected. In most situations, that leads to the bee's death. Only female bees are equipped with stingers, and all honeybee species (females) eventually die if they use their stinger because it's attached to the internal organs and cannot be dislodged safely without damaging them.

Storage Area

Bees use their abdomen to store the collected nectar and pollen. Nectar is the primary food source for bees, whereas pollen from flowers and trees contains other essential nutrients and proteins. The nectar and pollen are also transported to the colony, where bees and the younglings are fed.

Wax Glands

The wax gland is located in the bee's abdomen. As the name suggests, it is responsible for producing wax. The wax these glands make is used to make the hexagonal cells for their comb. In a beehive, the comb is a pivotal structure that serves as a communication medium between bees, provides an ideal space for brood rearing, and stores the food required for a bee colony to thrive.

Pollen Baskets

These concave structures are present on the hind legs and are used to transport pollen. Bees use these basket-like structures to collect and secure pollen with specialized hair, preventing the pollen from being wasted.

Pollen Brush

The pollen brush is the specialized hair present on the bees' legs. These bristled hairs act like brushes, collecting pollen from flowers, allowing the bee to fill their baskets.

The Lifecycle of Bees

The life cycle of honeybees is divided into four stages: egg, larva, pupa, and adult. Here's a brief explanation of each stage.

Egg Stage

The first stage starts with the queen bee laying fertilized eggs in the comb. The queen in the colony is the only female honeybee that reproduces. Other females in the colony are the direct offspring of the queen and act as worker bees. Likewise, male bees are called drones and reproduce with other females to start new colonies. Only male drones and female queens have developed reproductive systems. The queen bee in the egg stage lays a fertilized egg in each of the honeycombs and can easily lay around 3000 eggs a day.

Larva Stage

Larvae hatch from the eggs within three days. These legless larvae are dependent on adult worker bees (nursing bees) for care and nourishment. In the first two and a half days, the larva is fed royal jelly, a semi-solid substance rich in minerals, vitamins, and sugars, which provides them with the required nutrients to thrive. After feeding them royal jelly for a few days, the diet is switched to pollen and honey to let them recognize their ongoing food source. In the larva stage, the creature goes through five stages of larval instars. These stages represent the time when the larva sheds new skin as it grows in size.

Pupa Stage

After the fifth larval instar is complete, the larva transitions into the pupa stage. The larva then builds cocoons around themselves. In this stage, metamorphosis takes place. It's a biological process that occurs in the life cycle of most flying insects. Metamorphosis transforms the pupa into adult form in bees by making significant structural and physiological changes.

During this stage, body parts like the wings, antennae, compound eyes, and legs take shape, and several internal organs develop. Metamorphosis occurs over a period of a few days to weeks, depending on the bee species. The bee inside the cocoon stays dormant and uses the stored energy to develop the structures inside the hive.

Adult Stage

The emergence of the adult bee from the cocoon marks the completion of metamorphosis. The bees that leave the shell have comparatively soft bodies and crumpled wings. They make their wings expand and harden by pumping hemolymph into the wings, which comes from their own circulatory system. Over time, the exoskeleton of the bees hardens, providing the required support and protection.

As soon as the adult bee fully develops, they are assigned a role within their colony, according to the three castes, queens, drones, and workers. As mentioned, the worker bees are female and are the direct offspring of the queen but don't have fully developed reproductive systems to start a new colony. The worker bees can become nursing bees that care for the larva, take the role of cleaning the hive, gather pollen and nectar, construct the bee hive, and are always on the frontline when a threat is nearby.

The queen bees are the most prized caste in the beehive as the whole colony follows them. These bees release chemicals called pheromones that regulate the behavior of the others in the colony and influence their actions. Lastly, male bees or drones that don't have stingers are responsible for finding and mating with the queen to form another colony.

An adult bee's lifespan varies according to the time of year.

They might live a few weeks in the summer, but worker bees can survive for months in winter. Surprisingly, the lifespan of the queen can be as long as one or two years. Drones only live for a few weeks.

The Roles of Bees

In a colony, bees have distinct roles and responsibilities that contribute to the survival and functioning of the hive. The main castes of honeybees are the queen, worker bees, and drones. Here are the different roles and responsibilities of each caste:

Queen Bee

· **Egg Laying**

The queen bee's primary role is to lay eggs inside the honeycombs and ensure the colony thrives. On average, they can lay 3000 eggs daily, depositing individual eggs into a single honeycomb.

· **Pheromone Production**

The production of pheromones by the queen bees facilitates communication and improves the coordination and behavior of the remaining bees in the colony. These pheromones are crucial in maintaining the responsibilities of bees. For example, the released pheromones suppress the reproductive organs in female worker bees, which prevents them from reproducing.

- **Swarm Control**

Whenever the colony gets overcrowded, the queen bee can initiate the process of swarm control in which the new queen with several workers leaves in an attempt to build a new hive and expand. The queen bee is responsible for preparing the new queen and ensuring the expansion succeeds.

Worker Bees

Here are some of the responsibilities worker bees are assigned in a colony:

- **Nursing**

When the female offspring of the queen mature, they are given the nursing role. They are responsible for brooding and caring for the larvae the queen bee lays in the hive. Their glands also produce royal jelly, a nutritious substance that becomes the main source of nutrition for the developing larva. The nursing bees can also maintain the hive's internal temperature, ensure optimal development, and regulate the temperature in case it drops or rises too high.

- **Foragers**

One portion of worker bees acts as foragers, collecting nutritious nectar, pollen, and water. Some bees also collect propolis, a resin-like substance found in plants and trees.

· Builders and Architects

The worker bees are also responsible for maintaining the hive and expanding the colony. The beeswax their glands produce is used to craft intricate hexagonal shells in the honeycomb. Besides acting as a brooding ground for developing larvae, the honeycombs are used to store honey and pollen and maintain the structural integrity of the colony.

· Guards

The frontline of the hive is always the worker bees, as they are responsible for guarding the hive's entrance, identifying bees, and stopping predators and other insects from invading the colony.

· Undertakers

Several worker bees also act as undertakers, removing dead bees, debris, and other waste materials from the hive to maintain cleanliness and limit the spread of diseases. Without undertakers, maintaining hive hygiene is impossible.

· Hive Ventilation

Air circulation within the bee colony is necessary for it to thrive. The worker bees flutter their wings accordingly to control the humidity and temperature levels inside the hive, preventing overheating and ensuring optimal conditions are present for life to thrive in the colony.

Drones

- **Mating**

The major role of a drone is to mate with the new queens and to make and populate colonies. The drones have the shortest lifespan and usually die after mating in a few days.

- **Genetic Diversity**

Maintaining genetic diversity is imperative in a honeybee population. Drones increase genetic diversity by mating with queens from other colonies. This ensures better environmental adaptability and the long-term health of the bees.

It's imperative to understand that while these responsibilities are divided, they are not assigned indefinitely. The roles often change depending on the needs of the colony. Besides setting roles and using pheromones, bees communicate through various dances and other forms of bee communication to coordinate and execute effectively.

Maintaining the Hive

Bees employ various mechanisms and behaviors to maintain a healthy and productive hive. Here are some key factors that contribute to hive health and productivity:

· Hygienic Behavior

The bees have a natural hygienic behavior that protects against diseases and pests. Besides keeping harmful parasites and pathogens out of the honeycomb, worker bees regularly check the larva's health and scan them for the presence of parasites or pathogens. Whether it's an infection or a physical abnormality, worker bees can detect these issues and act immediately to remove the threat. The infected brood, debris, and dead bodies of other bees are regularly cleaned from the hive, ensuring hygiene and a thriving population.

· Propolis Collection

This resin is secreted from tree buds that the bees collect and carry to the hive for repairs. The worker bees use the collected propolis to seal cracks, fill crevices, and close small openings in the honeycomb. The material reinforces the hive surface and aids in limiting unwanted intruders from getting into the hive unnoticed. Propolis is antimicrobial and plays its part by limiting the growth of disease-causing microorganisms to proliferate.

· Foraging Efficiency

Foraging food is crucial for maintaining the hive; without food, the life cycle of the bees or virtually every other organism can cease to exist. Bees effectively collect foods like nectar and pollen and relay the location to other bees so they can join in with foraging. The bees also use distinct dance patterns and movements to communicate details about the food source, like the direction, distance, and quality. Other bees always follow the lead on the information they think is the best option to ensure the hive is maintained optimally.

· **Pollen Collection**

Bees collect nectar and pollen from flowers as essential sources of carbohydrates and proteins. They have specialized adaptations for efficient collection. They have a long proboscis (tongue) that allows them to reach the nectar deep within flowers. They also possess pollen baskets (corbiculae) on their hind legs. Bees pack the pollen into these baskets while foraging, enabling them to transport larger quantities back to the hive. By gathering both nectar and pollen, bees ensure a steady food supply for the colony.

Chapter Three

Chapter 3: Setting Up Your Apiary

In this chapter, you'll learn what an apiary is and why creating a suitable environment for your bees is essential. You'll also learn how to choose the right location and the importance of considering factors like access to nectar and pollen sources, water availability, and shelter from extreme weather conditions.

Apiaries: What You Should Know

To successfully train and care for honeybees, you must consider where to put them. After all, you can't keep them in your house. An apiary is where you should keep bees. It may differ from one place to another, depending on the location of the apiary and its structure.

Generally, a typical apiary does not involve the structure meant to house the bees alone but also the environment where it will be set, either temporarily or permanently.

Apiaries can be broadly divided into three major types.

1. Langstroth

The Langstroth beehive is a domesticated hive and is easily the most common apiary employed by beekeepers. For a good reason, this beehive has been around for over a hundred years.

It has three main sections:

· A lower section featuring a solid board of wood that supports the apiary
· Boxes where the rearing takes place and the honeybees are kept
· An upper section with an inner cover to secure the last box and an outer cover to seal the whole apiary from above

The peculiarities of the Langstroth beehive begin with its lower section, where the solid wood flooring has the entrance to the hive etched into the sides. This can also be replaced with a mesh net to serve as the bee entrance and provide adequate ventilation.

The Langstroth apiary uses various boxes, and new additions can be stacked on the less recent boxes. This feature makes this type of hive the highest honey-yielding out of all available options.

2. Warre

The Warre apiary is the new and improved form of the Langstroth. It is designed to simulate honeybees' natural environment and living conditions in the wild. It is finished in a manner that is bee-friendly and less stressful for the beekeeper to maintain.

The Warre is divided into:

· A base holding the weight of the apiary with the hive entrance situated on one side
· Boxes used to hold the bees, as well as their combs and honey
· A roof to protect the beehive from adverse weather conditions

The Warre differs from the Langstroth mainly in the size of its boxes, which are significantly smaller and make them unable to contain as much honey as the traditional Langstroth beehive. Also, differences can be spotted in how to expand the Warre apiary. Unlike the Langstroth, new boxes are added below the old ones.

3. Top Bar

The top bar hive is a modernized type designed to decrease the beekeeper's workload while providing the bees' necessities in seemingly natural settings. The Top Bar is made up of:

· Top bars, as the name implies, provide appropriate space between consecutive bee combs
· A top to cover the bees
· The box where the bees are kept, complete with an entrance and observation window

· Legs that lift the structure off the ground

The top bar hive is the most preferred of the three because bee combs are easy to remove, requiring just a knife at most. This apiary also only requires a little equipment to set up and maintain. Best of all, it allows for a quick inspection instead of lifting heavy boxes like what's needed with the Langstroth and Warre beehives. However, the top bar hive is non-expansible. It can only contain a fixed amount of bees.

Deciding the kind of apiary to employ in rearing your honeybees is important for several reasons:

· Maximizing the output of your honeybees
· Ensuring comfort and ease when maintaining your bees
· Ensuring that your expectations are met

Factors to Consider Before Setting Up an Apiary

An apiary goes beyond the housing structure. It also includes the environment where the bees are to be kept. For this reason, there is a need to critically analyze several factors situated around your preferred environment before erecting your beehive.

1. Food Availability

This is one of the most important factors to be looked into. While some beekeepers provide food for young bees in feeders, most mature worker bees will fly out of the hive and out of sight to look for food.

Honeybees feed on nectar and pollen, which are obtained from flowering plants. In erecting your apiary, you should consider any nearby garden, park, or farmyard with flowers to sustain your honeybees.

You should also find out if these plants are healthy enough to be consumed by the bees or if they were recently exposed to chemical agents like fertilizers and pesticides. You can decide to plant the yard housing your beehive with choice plants for your bees, depending on their species and preferences. This is safer, as you can account for what chemicals the plants have been exposed to.

2. Water Availability

Water is as essential to insects as it is to man. Bees with access to clean water produce clear honey of consistent thickness and color, while those without a good water source tend to produce honey with darker tones of brown.

When selecting the water source for your bees, test whether it's toxic. For example, water bodies running throughout farms might be tainted with insecticides, herbicides, and fertilizers. These chemicals could kill the bees or, worse, be present in the honey, ruining it entirely.

3. Hive Sustainability

Attempting to brood a large number of bees when you

have limited food and water sources in your immediate environment will ultimately fail because bees will not receive the same level of care throughout.

4. Spacing

Bees thrive when adequate space is provided; therefore, you need to consider spacing seriously. Good spacing between hives has been proven to drastically reduce the rate at which parasites and diseases spread between hives. Therefore, it is highly advised that a fair amount of distance is kept between hives.

5. Shelter

Before constructing your apiary, consider what additions you can put in place during the winter to make your bees comfortable. Think about what can be done in a rainstorm to protect the bees and the honey.

To solve a few of these problems, provide shade for the beehives in the form of trees or a small shed to provide coolness in extreme heat. Set windbreakers like trees surrounding your apiary to slow wind speed. Place roofs with comprehensive coverage over your apiary to prevent rain from reaching the hive.

6. Environmental risk

Before setting up a hive, you need to consider the risk factors your bees might pose and the hazards they face. For example, if a neighbor or relative is allergic to bee stings, consider setting up your hive in places where they can be affected. Also, if the fields around your home are constantly subject to chemical agents, consider what that will mean for your colonies.

7. Location

Ideally, a beehive will be located far from living spaces. However, city people are now rearing bees within neighborhoods.

You first need to check local laws to rear bees on your property. You should also check with your neighbors to see if they don't have a problem with it.

8. Access

You should also make sure that your apiary is easily accessed when needed. Access to your apiary is often overlooked during planning when in fact, it is a significant part of the process. An apiary that is not easily accessible will tire the beekeeper out, causing a drop in productivity. A drop in productivity will interfere with the apiary's routine maintenance and harvesting processes, causing significant inconvenience to the honey bees.

With that being said, an apiary stationed on a farm should be done so that equipment and bee products can be carried within walking range of a vehicle. If it is set in your homestead, it should be done so you can quickly go up for inspection at any time.

Equipment Needed to Set Up an Apiary

Once you are done analyzing and deciding the perfect spot for your apiary, it is time to set it up. This can be relatively easy, depending on the type of apiary you are setting up. This is relatively easy. The equipment you'll need includes:

1. Hive stand: This could be anything, ranging from a stack of bricks to an elaborate iron stand. Its primary purpose is to put some distance between the hive and the ground to prevent rot and cold transfer.

2. Feeders: These are provided for brooding bees before they go foraging for food.

3. Entrance reducer: This is mainly utilized in the Langstroth apiary to reduce the number of bees entering at any given time.

4. Queen excluder: This is a metal grid set to prevent or 'exclude' the queen from brooding into the honey to be harvested.

5. Smoker: This device produces smoke to calm the bees.

6. Quilt box: This box is designed to absorb moisture from your apiary during humid or cold weather. It could be filled with sawdust, burlap, and any material capable of absorbing moisture.

7. Beekeeper suit: This is essential to any beekeeper's closet. It is the protective material worn before attending to your honey bees.

8. Comb foundation sheet: This sheet simulates a bee comb and causes the bees to build theirs within the apiary.

9. Honey super: A honey super is essentially a box added to your apiary for your bees to store their honey. It is a superstructure, having eight to ten frames solely for holding honey.

10. Super clearer: These boards are placed beneath honey supers to rid the honeycomb of bees before harvesting.

11. Hive tool: This is the primary beekeeper tool. It is shaped like a hand-held scraper and is used in lifting frames, scraping off propolis, loosening stuck hive parts, and opening hive hatches. It is easily the most versatile equipment owned by an apiarist.

12. Pollen trap: This equipment is placed outside the entrance and used to trap pollen from incoming bees that may contaminate the honey.

Getting Honey Bees for Your Apiary

Apiary, check. Food and water, check. Location, check. All that remains is to acquire bees and place them in their new home.

There are four major ways you can obtain the bees you need. These are:

1. Buying a Nucleus Hive

A nucleus hive is by far one of the safest means of obtaining bees as a beginner. It consists of four to five bee frames containing starter bee combs and a few thousand bees with their queen. This hive, once bought, can just be placed in the brood box of your apiary and left alone to adjust to the new environment.

2. Buying Packaged Bees

Sounds funny, but yes, bees can be sent in packages. These sets of bees come without frames, so you must shake them from your package into your brood box and place frames to let them build their comb.

3. Splitting a Hive

This option suits people with friends or neighbors willing to share their honey bees with you. You might also be lucky enough to get a few starter frames, making your job easier. Splitting a hive is a good beekeeping practice, as it keeps the numbers small, preventing swarming.

4. Catching a Swarm

Catching a swarm of bees is an exhilarating experience that can yield great rewards for beekeepers. Although it is generally considered unsafe for inexperienced keepers, those with more experience can do it as long as they exercise caution. The process involves capturing a bee cluster that has left its original hive to establish a new colony.

When a swarm is spotted, it is essential to act swiftly and strategically. First, the beekeeper must be properly equipped with protective clothing, including a beekeeping suit, gloves, and a veil. They should also have the necessary tools, such as a hive box, frames, and a bee brush.

Approaching the swarm calmly and gently, the beekeeper can encourage the bees to cluster on a branch, fence, or other convenient surface. Carefully, they will shake or brush the bees into the prepared hive box, ensuring the queen bee is included. The queen's scent will attract the other bees and encourage them to enter the box.

Once most bees are inside the hive box, the beekeeper can seal it and transport it to its new location. Handling the swarm carefully and minimizing any stress or disruption to the bees during the process is crucial.

Setting up your apiary might test your will to continue as a beekeeper, from deciding the perfect hive for you to setting it up to bring in your bees. However, with the help and tips in this chapter, you should be able to decide what type of apiary would suit your needs.

Chapter Four

Chapter 4: Hive Management and Honey Production

Hive maintenance is an important part of beekeeping. You must pay close attention to your bees' well-being by proactively caring for their hives. Proper management makes all the difference when it comes to making high-value returns. In this chapter, you will learn about hive management, its techniques, and their importance. You will also learn about the seasonal factors to consider, including feeding and prep work of your hive during the winter and summer seasons. Additionally, the chapter covers several techniques and practices that can maximize your honey production, all while prioritizing your hive's well-being.

The Importance of Hive Management

Practicing sound beekeeping methods provides many

advantages, including maintaining a healthy honeybee colony and generating various beehive products. For environmentally-conscious beekeepers, mastering effective management techniques means fostering the growth of sizable colonies that can easily be divided and expected to swarm multiple times naturally. Ultimately, the primary benefits of adopting good beehive management practices include the following:

1. Excellent Yields

Beekeepers who are both prudent and insightful often report impressive gains on an annual basis, mainly thanks to successfully managing their hives. By utilizing sound strategies, they can produce valuable products like honey, royal jelly, beeswax, and propolis, which are highly profitable through trade within the industry. These experienced beekeepers often divide their beehives into multiple packages that they can then sell to new farmers looking for opportunities in honeybee breeding. This production of a good amount of top-quality products within a given time frame proves essential in maintaining a successful apiary business model that assures profitability over time and allows for further expansion with ease.

2. Improved Bee Health

The preservation of bee colonies stands out as a crucial component when successfully managing hives. Proper management of bees and their colonies increases their ability to withstand varying challenges like diseases, pests, and unfavorable climatic conditions, among many others.

Therefore, beekeepers must regularly examine to identify any signs indicating possible infections or infestations and implement timely intervention measures. This will help boost the chances of averting disasters and increase the possibility of healthier beehives, achievable with good nutrition and proper pollen management.

3. Learning and Development

Aspiring beekeepers with a passion for mastering the art of apiculture stand to gain many benefits by applying excellent hive management methods. Bees are fascinating creatures whose behavioral nuances vary from season to season, and by closely observing them over time, you will learn a great deal about their needs and preferences, along with identifying any stressors that may exist in their environment. By intentionally keeping hives healthy through thoughtful intervention strategies, any aspiring beekeeper will succeed tremendously in this rewarding field.

4. Protecting the Natural Environment

Are you aware that protecting natural environments requires effective hive management practices? Due to their role as primary pollinators for many plant species and flowers, your honeybees play a central role in protecting and maintaining the stability of the natural environment. So, you have to properly manage hives by promoting healthy bee populations, which is critical to successful pollination and leads to a healthier environment and a thriving ecosystem. In turn, this approach preserves habitats and supports broad-scale environmental sustainability efforts by guaranteeing biodiversity.

5. Monetary Rewards

For beekeepers seeking financial gains from their trade, proper hive management practices are vital to achieving this specific objective. Successfully implementing these management practices will result in increased yields which will also translate into greater earning potential through direct sales channels or partnerships. Moreover, prioritizing the health and welfare of your bees guarantees higher quality standards that will resonate with consumers seeking excellent pure honey products. If you follow this model of sustainable business growth within the apiary farming system, the potential returns will exceed what you expect from normal market scenarios, and the impact it will have on customer satisfaction goes beyond loyalty and positive image-building.

6. Reduced Stress

There is a vital link between effectively managing bee colonies and promoting a healthy environment for them. When you adopt proper practices in your beehive management, you create a conducive atmosphere that guarantees calmness and high productivity levels. On the other hand, when their habitat gets disrupted, honeybees become aggressive, resulting in low success rates in the production and expansion of bee colonies. Unfortunately, when things go too far due to internal or external disturbances like human intervention or intrusions on their territory by pests or diseases, there's no other way for them but to flee and look for new shelter elsewhere.

Best Management Practices

As a serious beekeeper, you must always be ready to identify signs of tension within a hive and promptly intervene. Whether you're a beginner or an experienced beekeeper, handling stressed colonies involves utilizing several effective approaches that deal with current and potential issues. Moreover, by intentionally implementing specific hive management practices designed to minimize anxiety levels, you can provide optimal care for your bees. Some such helpful management strategies include:

1. Keeping an Eye on Your Bees

Try your best to prioritize the health and protection of your bee population by staying vigilant about the activities within the hive. To do that, you should regularly conduct thorough hive inspections. Inspecting hives every one to two weeks during active seasons is an excellent way to detect diseases within the colony while also checking for the queen bee's presence and assessing overall colony strength. By consistently monitoring your bees and their needs, you can prevent issues with brood patterns or honey storage and respond promptly to any problems.

2. Identifying and Addressing Hive Stressors through Inspection

Casual observation alone when hive tension sources are

difficult to determine is not enough. Beekeepers must look even deeper. Thorough examinations allow for a more comprehensive understanding of pressing issues affecting colonies amid challenges like disease outbreaks or changes in climate patterns. If you don't pay enough attention when identifying what is wrong with your colonies, you risk picking false solutions, which can impact the bee population.

3. Pests and Diseases Control

Promptly acknowledging any signs of diseases, pests, or parasites within your beehive is another important management practice to maintain your bee colonies' well-being. Treating different illnesses can be done using various methods and compounds. Higher costs associated with specific treatments should not prevent you from implementing the appropriate measures. Using effective techniques that are suitable and easily obtainable proves helpful when tackling pests or parasites. For example, small hive beetles and wax moths often stress bees. Varroa mites also have a significant chance of affecting hives. Thoracic mites pose severe threats that can also negatively impact the bees.

4. Temperature Control

Honeybees play a significant role in maintaining the natural ecosystem. For bees, the optimal living conditions are around 35 degrees Celsius. During harsh winter months, bees bundle up together to survive before returning to their traditional way of life during spring. Summer months present a unique risk where bees may suffer from overheating. They respond to heat by coordinating water droplet evaporation and optimizing airflow inside the hive. Extreme weather patterns can negatively affect productivity and health, resulting in declining honeybee populations worldwide. Beekeepers can prevent the negative consequences of that with straightforward solutions like temporary shading or insulation.

5. Keeping Your Bees Together

Swarming contributes to the proliferation of bee colonies and boosts reproduction. However, this behavior can lead to reduced numbers of bees and weaker hives overall. You should maintain appropriate space within the hive by incorporating extra brood boxes while carrying out periodic checks for swarm cells without fail. If required, dividing the colony can also help sustain stable bee populations.

6. Ventilation

Proper ventilation within the hive is necessary for maintaining an ideal temperature, adequate humidity levels, and good air quality. Accumulation of carbon dioxide released during breathing cycles combined with body heat could cause various issues if left unchecked. Aim to keep your bee's environment comfortable by installing screened bottom boards with upper entrances or adding carefully positioned ventilation holes to promote good airflow.

7. Nourishing the Bees

Consistent nourishment is essential in fostering healthy bee colonies throughout the year. When nectar is scarce (commonly during winter or early spring), you can supplement it with either sugar syrup or fondant so that they remain well-fed and healthy. Additionally, placing feeders next to the brood area and keeping tabs on food consumption can ensure that your precious bees do not suffer from inadequate nutrition that can lead to starvation or even death.

8. Choosing a Good Spot

When tending to honeybees, providing them with optimal living space is essential for their growth and welfare. So, when searching for possible hive locations, bear in mind how sunlight might impact them whilst shielding them against gusty winds if possible.

Raising the colonies above ground level can assist in controlling humidity and offering uninterrupted bee movement in all directions. Always avoid selecting areas that are regularly treated with pesticides.

9. Taking care of the Queen

As the driving force behind any hive, the role of the queen bee cannot be understated, especially since she guarantees regular egg-laying activity that preserves population stability over time. Paying close attention to your queen's health status and work functionality are key success factors when aiming to maintain strong hive bearings. Key elements that should be observed include healthy brood development patterns, gentle mannerisms with other bees in support roles, and good physical stamina. Swap underperforming queens with fit younger ones where necessary to prevent any decline in productivity.

10. Collecting honey

If a beekeeper wants to assist their bees in obtaining additional honey, they can choose to incorporate supplementary supers into the hive configuration. Honey levels must be regularly monitored, and new supers should be added accordingly as the bee colony expands. When all frames have become full and properly sealed with wax caps, the unprocessed honey-rich rewards have matured enough for removal.

11. Keeping Records

Anyone involved in beekeeping knows that maintaining careful records is essential for success. Doing so involves keeping a detailed hive diary where you note important aspects like inspections, honey yields, and pest treatments. This allows you to effectively analyze trends over time, ultimately leading to informed decision-making in the future based on these insights gleaned from past performance data points. Use organizational skills while leveraging digital tools or specialized apps as necessary to organize record-keeping and streamline efficiency along the way.

12. Staying Ahead

As a beekeeper, you must remain ahead of the curve by constantly educating yourself on the latest industry standards and embracing them through professional development opportunities, like local meetups or online discussion portals dedicated to sharing practical knowledge. Adopting the best possible practices enables beekeepers to address cross-functional challenges successfully.

Maximizing Honey Production

Factors like species or breeding practices can affect yields. A sought-after baseline average observed globally among experienced beekeepers is approximately 40 pounds per hive annually, which ultimately depends on external factors. Differences between growing seasons duration or habitat conditions alongside other influencing variables that skilled farmers accommodate into individualized methods capable of netting up to 100 pounds per hive.

1. Increasing Beehive Space

For beekeepers looking to make the best of honey production, providing your honeybees extra space is a crucial element to help achieve this objective. You must take care not to jeopardize hive security by creating an opening for pests and predators. An additional box will not only help the bees produce more honey, but it will also minimize swarming possibilities. During the nectar-flow period, the timely addition of super boxes continues to be key as it gives bees adequate room for boosting their operations of generating adequate and pleasant fluid. Moreover, during this period, you can remove the structures completely covered with honey and return them to the beehive before the period ends.

2. Growing Flowering Plants

The findings gathered through biological studies confirm the indispensable role played by surrounding flora in accommodating the nutritional requirements of bees. Bees acquire much of their nutrition from nectar and pollen. Consequently, planting flowers nearby is suggested as it gives bees access to a bountiful supply of ideal food resources throughout their collection process. A varied series of plants composed largely of wide flowering plants are helpful given that bees have little proboscises, unable to access plants requiring more pressure or bigger entryways.

3. Incorporating Security Measures

- **Hive Placement:** Select a secure and secluded location for the hive, away from potential disturbances such as heavy foot traffic, animals, or extreme weather conditions. This helps reduce the risk of vandalism or accidental damage.

- **Fencing:** Installing a sturdy fence around the hive can act as a barrier, deterring large animals or unauthorized individuals from getting too close to the bees. Make sure the fence is constructed in a way that allows for proper ventilation and hive access.

- **Hive Entrance Protection**: To prevent unwanted intruders, such as predators or robber bees, consider implementing an entrance reducer. This reduces the size of the hive entrance, making it easier for bees to defend against intruders while maintaining the colony's security.

- **Monitoring and Surveillance:** Set up a monitoring system, such as security cameras or motion sensors, near the hive to keep an eye on any suspicious activity or potential threats. Regularly review the footage to identify any issues and take appropriate action if necessary.

- **Pest Management:** Implement effective pest management strategies to control common hive pests like Varroa mites or hive beetles. Regularly inspect the hive for signs of infestation and take appropriate measures, such as using natural treatments or integrated pest management techniques, to keep the colony protected.

- **Educate and Inform**: Raise awareness in your local community about the importance of bees and the need for hive security. Encourage your neighbors to respect the hive's boundaries and inform them about the potential consequences of interfering with it.

By incorporating these security measures, beekeepers can create a safe environment for their bees, reduce the risk of disturbances or threats, and promote the well-being and productivity of the colony.

Beekeeping success depends on competent hive management, which emphasizes focusing on routine evaluations, seeing that there is year-round food readily available, keeping a cautious watch on parasites and conditions, and thinking about seasonal effects on swarm behavior. Being consistent with these habits will make them second nature to you. Strategies like flock avoidance mechanisms, employment of integrated bug control strategies, queen reproduction techniques, and hive splitting treatments are all essential components adding to general beehive well-being. When carried out properly, these techniques can go a long way in supporting your beekeeping endeavors.

Chapter Five

Chapter 5: Beekeeping Safety and Disease Management

A big part of beekeeping is caring for the bees and keeping them safe from diseases and environmental threats. Also, adequate safety measures reduce the risk of bee stings or allergic reactions. The safety gear you wear is the first line of defense between you and the bees. It includes a beekeeping suit, a mesh veil, boots, and gloves that keep you protected at all times during hive inspection and maintenance.

Masking Pheromones

Beekeepers continually seek better methods to ensure the well-being of their bees during hive management. One effective technique employed is the use of bee smoke, which effectively conceals the bee pheromones emitted by the queen bee to alert other bees of potential intrusion. By masking these pheromones, the smoke reduces aggressiveness, minimizing the risk of stinging and ensuring safe handling of the hive.

Making Slow Movements

Handling the bees is crucial when tending to the honeycomb or extracting honey or other bee products. Making slow movements will reduce the chances of you appearing as a threat.

Regular Inspections

You should regularly check the hive for potential diseases. Any signs of diseases or pest infestations are evident and can be detected with the right knowledge.

Having the required knowledge about the diseases honeybees are susceptible to is necessary. Having this information makes it easier for you to make an effective action plan and ensure the health and productivity of the bee colony.

Go Green

Different pesticides and chemicals in the market can be used to control the spread of pests and bee-related diseases. However, the modern-day beekeeper prefers to keep it all green. Nowadays, beekeepers use the integrated pest management approach that focuses on controlling pests through a mix of chemical, natural, and traditional methods while minimizing the use of pesticides. Implementing this strategy protects the bee's health, provides pest-free by-products, and minimizes environmental impact.

Keeping It Clean

Maintaining a beehive involves using several tools. They should be cleaned and sanitized after each use. The gear you wear should also be cleaned and disinfected after each time. Using clean tools reduces the chances of disease or pest transmission to the hive.

Location of the Colony

You can't just start a bee colony anywhere. Selecting the right location is crucial. Look for areas where nature is thriving and relatively untouched by humans. For example, you can create an artificial ecosystem where you can plant various flowers and green plants that support the overall health and productivity of the bees. Avoid picking areas with pollutants and pesticides.

Following adequate safety measures, conducting regular inspections, and expanding your knowledge of beekeeping safety can keep you and your bees safe, healthy, and productive.

Safety Gear

Your safety gear is the first line of defense and provides the necessary protection against bee stings and subsequent allergies or flare-ups.

Beekeeping Suit

The beekeeping suit provides a full body cover and is the

most basic piece of safety gear. There are several variations of these suits; some are in the form of a jacket, whereas others resemble a hazmat suit. The suit is loosely woven using a thick fabric that acts as a barrier and prevents the bees from reaching the skin.

Ensure that the suit you buy fits appropriately and isn't too loose or tight to allow for comfortable movement.

Veil

The veil attached to the beekeeping suit protects the face and neck against stings. A mesh-like, fine material allows the beekeeper to see clearly, keeping the bees away from the skin. The veil can be attached to the hat or worn separately.

The straps of the veil should be properly secured to prevent the bees from entering from the neck area. Lastly, regularly check your veil and the suit for tears, as the mesh-like material used to make the gear can wear out with regular use.

Gloves

You'll need a pair of beekeeping-compatible gloves to protect your hands and wrists. These gloves are usually made from thick rubber or leather, which protects against bee stings. The material is also easy to clean and sanitize, making it an excellent pick for beekeepers.

Always go for a pair that fits perfectly in your hands and that don't restrict natural hand movements. Only wear the gloves after putting on the suit, and ensure the cuffs are tucked inside the glove. Doing so will prevent bees from entering the suit from gaps between the gloves and sleeves. While wearing gloves is always recommended, experienced beekeepers can be seen handling bees without them, as they believe that they can decrease tactile sensitivity.

Boots

Beekeeping boots are explicitly designed to cover the feet, ankles, and lower leg area to ensure that bees don't slip through crevices in the feet or ankle areas. Traditionally, the boots are made of leather, but there are also slip-resistant rubber boots with a high shaft for bee-sting protection. Try them on when purchasing the boots, see whether they fit well, and keep your feet comfortable. Like gloves, you'll wear these boots over the beekeeping suit.

Always ensure that the safety gear you use doesn't have any tears, should fit properly and that all the tools you use are inspected and cleaned after each use. Regular cleaning will prevent the transmission of any diseases. Besides sanitizing the gear, store everything in a clean and dry place. As you work on protecting yourself, it's also crucial to gather knowledge about bee-handling techniques and the protocols to follow to prevent the bees from getting agitated and exhibiting defensive or aggressive behavior.

Hive-Handling Techniques

Using gentle handling techniques is paramount and can

prevent the bees from becoming stressed. When implemented perfectly, these techniques keep the bees in harmony and prevent them from seeing you as a threat.

Making Slow Movements

Learn and practice the art of slow and deliberate movements for maximum effectiveness. If you exhibit jerky movements, the bees might perceive the motion as a threat, putting the colony on high alert. Make graceful hand movements and stay calm.

Bee Smoke

Moderately using bee smoke is one of the most effective ways to control their behavior. This can be a beekeeper's best tool when used effectively. The smoke calms them down. Before opening the hive for inspection or management, apply a few puffs of smoke near and around the entrance. The smoke acts as a veil that will mask the pheromones queen bees produce to alarm other bees.

It's always recommended to use smoke in moderation, especially when you have just started beekeeping. Over time, as you gain experience, you'll know the amount of bee smoke to use, as overdoing it can create the opposite effect. It will make the bees agitated.

Proper control and application require time and will come naturally as you progress and gain experience. Beekeepers who are new to the field make the common mistake of blowing smoke directly inside the entrance while pointing at the bees. The smoke should cover the hive slightly, not fill it up entirely and suffocate the bees.

Time It Right

In the beekeeping world, timing your moves is necessary. You can't rush in whenever, open up the hive for inspection, or maintain it whenever you like. You'll need to stick to a set of rules. The best time is when the weather conditions are calm and favorable. For example, inspecting the hive on a windy or rainy day can agitate the bees. Warm and sunny days are perfect for hive inspection and management.

Handling with Care

When accessing the frames and comb, handle them with the utmost care, as these can easily get damaged and deformed with the slightest pressure.

When inspecting or replacing frames, minimizing the time a hive stays exposed is important. The bees always work in complete harmony, which can be disrupted when the hive is unnecessarily exposed open. As a beekeeper, it's your responsibility to respect their environment and avoid peeking into the hive out of curiosity when you won't be doing any maintenance. After you inspect the hive, make sure to seal it back up properly. Everything needs to fit in perfectly and be properly secured. Seeing how hives are naturally dark inside, even a tiny opening can disrupt their behavior.

Whenever you interact with the bees and the colony, see it as an opportunity to learn something new and focus on treating the bees respectfully. You might have seen those videos on social media where beekeepers are covered in bees. Although it's never recommended to attempt something like this, these demonstrations show that the bees don't do any harm when they are calm.

Common Diseases That Affect Bees

Like any other living thing, bees can get affected by several diseases and pests. That can impact their health, well-being, and hive functioning, even putting their integrity at stake. Some common diseases you should know about bees include the following:

Varroosis (Varroa Mites)

It's one of the most common diseases affecting honeybees. Parasitic in nature, varroosis is caused by Varroa mites which lodge themselves into the bee to suck their hemolymph. Think of these mites as leeches. They slowly weaken the bees and act as a vector for five viruses that transmit instantly, jeopardizing the whole bee colony.

The most evident signs of Varroa mite infestation include deformed wings, mites lodged on the bee's body, perforated pupae, or seeing the mites on the hive surface. Following pest management protocols is necessary to control and mitigate the infestation. Using thyme essential oil, screened bottom boards, and regularly inspecting the bees are ways to keep the mite levels in check.

American Foulbrood (AFB)

This highly contagious bacterial disease is caused by Penibacillus larvae that spread by forming spores. The spores directly affect the bee larva. After successful infestation, the spores spread quickly within the hive, infecting the remaining larvae. When you inspect them, you'll see sunken, greasy-looking, dark brood cells with perforations. To confirm the presence of AFB, light a matchstick and insert it into one of the larva cells and the infected brood will rope out.

Contacting disease management authorities is necessary to ensure the spread is contained. You'll need to destroy the hive by burying or burning the infected area.

European Foulbrood (EFB)

The bacterium Melissococcus is the culprit behind the European Foulbrood disease. It's similar to AFB as it only affects the bee larva but is less intense. The larvae infected with EFB have discolored and twisted bodies, making it nearly impossible for them to transition to the pupa stage. You'll see dead and elongated larvae and perforated brood openings. Unlike AFB, EFB doesn't produce a foul or rotting smell.

The root cause of most diseases affecting the larva is poor hygiene. Other factors include the queen's scarcity of good nutrition, stress, or poor management. Changing the queen is one practical method to strengthen the weak colony while ensuring their nutritional needs are met.

Stonebrood

This is a fungal disease caused by an Aspergillus fungus. The disease weakens the colony by killing the brooding larvae and limiting the colony to growth. The affected larvae look like small stones and have a chalky appearance. The larvae will crumble when touched, confirming the presence of stonebrood. Removing affected hive areas is necessary to control the spread, besides providing adequate nutrition and hygiene.

Deformed Wing Virus

This viral disease affects the wings of adult bees, making them crippled, deformed, and unable to fly. The Varroa mites mentioned earlier are a vector for this virus. You can easily identify DWV, as most adult bees will have deformed wings, short abdomens, and distorted body parts. The affected colony needs to be eradicated to prevent the spread of the virus to other nearby bee colonies. Furthermore, controlling the mite population is also imperative to control the spread.

Nosema

Nosema is a fungal disease caused by the microsporidian parasites Nosema apis and Nosema ceranae. These parasites infect the intestinal tracts of adult bees and can impact their digestive system, leading to a reduced lifespan, weakened immune response, and diminished colony productivity.

Upon inspection, you won't find any apparent changes in the bee colony or the hive. Lab tests are necessary to confirm the presence of Nosema within the colony. After noticing decreased productivity in the bee colony, adult bees are tested for the parasite. This parasitic infection can be managed by strengthening the immune system through good nutrition and assisting the bees in keeping the hive hygienic. However, if you see no improvements, it's best to consult a parasite control expert for bees to execute a management strategy.

Chalkbrood

Chalkbrood is a fungal disease caused by the fungus Ascosphaera apis. It primarily affects bee larvae and transforms them into chalk-like mummies. Infected larvae turn white and harden, which eventually leads to their death. Although chalkbrood does not usually cause widespread colony losses, severe infestations can weaken colonies.

The larvae in this fungal disease die and take on a chalk-like appearance. You'll see mummified dead larvae near the entrance and at the hive's bottom. Proper ventilation is imperative to prevent it from spreading, as high humidity levels promote fungal growth. Expert beekeepers also recommend replacing the queen bee with a healthier one and replacing or removing the affected areas of the colony.

Sacbrood

Sacbrood is a viral disease that affects bee larvae, primarily the youngest ones. It is caused by the Sacbrood virus (SBV) and leads to larval death. Infected larvae appear swollen, with their bodies elongated and twisted. While sacbrood can impact individual hives, it generally does not cause extensive damage to the entire colony.

When inspecting the hive, the larvae affected by the disease appear swollen and have elongated bodies. Unlike their pearly white color, the affected larvae turn brown, resembling a fluid-filled sac. Sacbrood will go away on its own without any intervention. However, it's necessary to maintain good hive hygiene and provide good nutrition so the bees can better fight the disease.

Chronic Bee Paralysis Virus (CBPV)

This is a viral disease that affects adult bees. The most apparent symptoms of the virus include hair loss in bees, erratic shaking, and losing the ability to fly. CBPV can spread quickly within a colony, deteriorating its functionality and overall health.

The Varroa mites mentioned earlier are a carrier of this viral disease. If a specific course of treatment is not made, you need to monitor their health closely and call a professional if you see the colony's health deteriorating rapidly.

There are several other health conditions, like the Israeli Acute Paralysis virus, Kashmir bee virus, lethal brood disease, and acariasis, that can affect the health of the bees. Reading more about these diseases and intervening before it's too late is key. Although it's your responsibility to regularly inspect the hive and keep an eye out if you see any signs of disease, a certified bee specialist should always carry out a diagnosis and adequate management by following the lead of an experienced beekeeper.

Chapter Six

Chapter 6: Harvesting Honey

Most people get into beekeeping to produce honey. There are many benefits associated with beekeeping; you can connect to your environment, boost plant pollination in your area, and enjoy homegrown honey. Knowing the necessary steps and time for harvesting honey from your beehive is imperative. Before you proceed with the extraction, you should ask yourself: how do I harvest honey from a beehive? When is the right time to extract it? How do I keep it fresh during storage?

As a novice beekeeper, the idea of extraction can be exciting, but knowing the right tools and ways to extract your honey can be overwhelming. However, this chapter will prepare you for your first harvest. You will learn how to determine the right timing, the best methods and ways to store and preserve it after you extract it for safe use, and tips on how to filter and identify the right containers for preservation. Honey extraction can be messy, but rest assured, it's easy to pull off once you know what to do. Just make sure you have the right tools.

When to Harvest Honey

One way to know the best time to harvest is to look out for flower blooms. Flowers bring nectar, and nectar leads to honey. The best time to harvest honey is around June and July, when flowers bloom. In spring, flowers don't bloom as much, leading to less honey. Study flowers in and out of their seasons for the best honey harvesting results. Other key indicators are:

Bee Behaviour

The role of bees and their behaviors in determining if honey is ready to be harvested cannot be overemphasized. When bees sense that the moisture content of the honey is low enough, they cap the surface with wax. Doing this preserves its quality. To know that the honey is ready, all you have to do is watch and observe.

Capped Honeycomb Cells

Capping is what bees do to seal mature honey. They do this to preserve the moisture content, which should usually be around 17-18%. So, while you inspect the hive, watch out for capped honeycombs, as this is a sign that the honey is ready to be harvested.

Overall, Colony Strength

A strong colony of bees gets you a healthy amount of bee

workers, ensuring a healthy amount of honey. Make sure that the hive has sustained a good amount of honey before you think of harvesting. However, delaying harvesting is wise in this instance if you don't think there is enough honey.

How to Harvest Your Honey

1. Crush and Strain

You can build a foundation for collecting honey with a simple wax or plastic. First, scrape your honeycomb out of the plastic into a strainer. Afterward, you can squeeze or cut the honeycomb until the cells open. The process is continued until all honey is dried out of the honeycomb. You can then filter and bottle it up. You can use a container and a colander to strain and capture the honey or use ready-made tools specifically designed to extract honey.

How can you create a strainer for extraction? Get two five-gallon plastic buckets. Drill tiny holes at the bottom of the first bucket to prevent the wax from falling through. Cut through the center to the top for the second bucket and leave an inch of the lower part. Then, place the drilled bucket on it. When the wax is strained, the rest of the honey falls into the lower lid, and then, you can bottle it for use. When you're done with the process, set aside the leftover wax so the bees can collect the rest of the honey and preserve it for the next harvest.

2. Extractor

Extractors are centrifugal-like devices that use force to extract honey from a comb's frames. The honey extracted here flows directly into your jar and is ready for use. Consider using this device if your harvest weighs more than five colonies. You can also use it for lesser numbers, but using a honey extractor for larger numbers helps you save time and energy.

A usual honey extractor has a cylinder or drum-like container (stainless steel), and this has both radial and tangential kinds of setup within the extractor where you can place your honeycomb frames and begin extraction. The radial setup extracts honey from both comb sides simultaneously, but the former does just one side. Extractors are very reliable for commercial purposes, and with a spigot close to the bottom of the machine, you can open and access all the honey stored there.

How does the extraction work?

You can start the extraction after harvesting the mature honeycombs. You get your matured honeycombs by carefully selecting specific frames ready for harvesting. Ensure you're fully protected from this extraction because you wouldn't want to do this step without being safe. Ensure the bees are removed as you transfer the frames into a closed or sealed container that no insect or bee can access. When you're in a safe space away from the bees, use a heated spoon or knife to scrape the wax off the frames carefully. After that, you can place the frames into the honey extractor.

Press the "on" button if it's an electric extractor to get the machine to vibrate. Repeat the process for all the other frames and get ready for bottling and storage. Compared to the comb and strain extraction method, this one is fast and easy.

Why use an extractor? One great advantage of using a honey extractor is that it leaves the cells of your honeycomb intact. The only thing you have to do is to remove the wax.

3. Comb Honey

This method produces the kind of honey people are okay with paying quite a bit of money to get. For this method, you can use frames instead of plastic as the foundation for your honey. Cut your honeycombs from the frames, then cut those frames into smaller chunks, after which you can package them in a jar or container. With this method, you get to eat the comb along with the honey. It's efficient and easy and doesn't require uncapping the honey.

According to Richard Taylor, author of "The Comb Honey Book," there is a widespread misconception that it'll take bees a long time to build up honeycombs when they are discarded or consumed and that with readily available combs, made available through extractors, it saves bees the trouble of starting anew. This is only partly true.

During seasons when nectars of flowers are flourishing, bees make the most amount of wax. This factor is independent of the availability of combs to build on. It doesn't matter if wax is available or not. Honey and wax depend on the amount of nectar available to bees. If bees do not use the nectar to build combs, it goes to waste.

How to Safely Store Honey

Now that you've extracted your honey, what next? After extraction, you use a double sieve to drain your honey. If you're the type of person that prefers honey pure and without any comb, you should do this. The steps below are how you can bottle, package, and store honey:

· Make sure to use a clean container for storage. Honey can be stored for so long without going bad. The biggest reason it goes wrong is when it is contaminated, which can happen through dirty equipment during preparation and storage. After years of storage, a honey jar can have the same quality and taste.

· Use glass jars. Plastic does not guarantee your safety, as some plastics can leak chemicals and add unpleasant odors to honey. Whereas glass prevents moisture from getting in, therefore increasing its shelf life.

· Watch out for moisture. Honey can last for years, but only if stored in the right environment. The preferable moisture percentage is from 17-18%. Anything above or below can lead to spoilage. The bees indeed reduce the moisture level of the honey by introducing wax. That is why local beekeepers store honey in closed rooms with dehumidifiers to ensure stable moisture levels.

Storing Honey for Personal Use

Are you in search of something affordable and easy to use? Try:

· Small Sized Canning Jars

These containers are cheap and easy to get and are the perfect-sized jars for any pantry. They are also the perfect shape for reheating honey. These quart-sized jars can fit approximately three pounds of honey. You can use these for short-term storage.

· Recycled Jars

Using recycled jars can be a great way to save costs. However, before using them, make sure that you thoroughly clean and disinfect them. Failing to do so can lead to a sour taste and even spoilage. It's safer to skip this type of container and use it for another storage purpose.

· Half Sizes Gallon Jars

A typical glass gallon jar of honey weighs around 12 pounds. Since that can be too heavy for most people, it's recommended that you use half-size gallon jars. They are easy to manage and store.

Storing Honey for Long Term

When storing honey long-term, you want it to avoid absorbing moisture by properly sealing it. If you plan on storing raw honey, do so below 50°F and avoid exposing it to sunlight.

Tips for Filtering and Bottling Honey

It's essential that you properly filter and bottle your honey. Follow these tips to do just that:

· Make sure that your storage equipment is properly sterilized before use.

· Before storing your extracted honey in jars, allow it to sit for a day or two to allow air bubbles to surface. Remove any floating cells or dirt that may have entered when it took to settle.

· Use the right filter size: As you prepare to store your honey in clean jars, use the appropriate size of filters. A 200-400 micron of filter does a good job of preventing small particles like pollen grains from entering.

· Bottle and label the honey: Use high-quality jars for bottling. As you fill the bottles, leave a small room at the top for changes in texture due to temperature fluctuations. Wipe off any excess on the container's body and seal it with airtight lids. Don't forget to label honey according to its rawness and preservation dates. Then, store in a cool and dry place. Regularly inspect the honey to make sure there is no spoilage or fermentation.

There is no honey without bees. As a beekeeper, harvesting honey takes much more than just taking down frames from a beehive. In addition, you now know the right time to harvest honey, the best methods, and the safest way to preserve it for daily and long-term use.

Harvesting honey culminates the hard work and dedication put into beekeeping. However, you need to remember that honey production is intricately tied to the bees' well-being. Beekeepers understand that harvesting honey goes beyond simply collecting frames from a beehive; it requires careful consideration and respect for the bees' needs and the overall health of the colony.

Timing plays a crucial role here too. Beekeepers must assess the hive's strength, ensuring the colony has ample honey reserves to sustain itself through winter. Harvesting too early can leave the bees without sufficient food, jeopardizing their survival. By monitoring the hive's honey stores and understanding the local nectar flow, beekeepers can determine the ideal time to harvest, striking a balance between the bees' needs and honey production.

Once the honey is ready for harvest, beekeepers employ various methods to extract it from the comb. This can include using specialized tools like honey extractors or employing traditional methods such as crush, strain, or cut comb. Each technique has advantages and considerations, allowing beekeepers to choose the best way for their preferences and resources.

Proper preservation is crucial after the honey is extracted to maintain its quality and flavor. Beekeepers employ safe and hygienic methods to filter the honey, removing impurities while preserving its natural properties. It is then carefully stored in clean, airtight containers, protecting it from moisture and contaminants. Properly preserved honey can be enjoyed daily or stored for long-term use, allowing beekeepers to savor the fruits of their labor throughout the year.

This chapter has emphasized the interdependence between bees and honey production. Beekeepers understand that their role extends beyond honey extraction; it encompasses the care and well-being of the bees, ensuring their health and vitality for future honey harvests. By adopting sustainable and bee-friendly practices, beekeepers play a vital role in preserving these remarkable creatures and the invaluable honey they provide.

Chapter Seven

Chapter 7: Beyond Honey: Other Bee Products

In the beekeeping world, honey is not the only by-product you should focus on harvesting. Various products include beeswax, royal jelly, bee bread, bee pollen, and propolis. From candle-making and making woodworking polishes to improving vitality and health, these versatile and natural by-products are a treasure for the beekeeper. This chapter will briefly explore the fantastic products you can access when beekeeping.

Beeswax

This natural substance is the basic material that makes the hives. Beeswax is produced by specialized glands present in the abdomen of worker bees. The secreted wax is in the form of thin scales which worker bees chew and manipulate using their jaws, making it pliable and easy to mold into hexagonal cells.

This substance is composed of long-chain fatty acids, esters, and almost 300 other compounds. The composition of the secreted beeswax changes with the bee's diet and environmental changes. However, their physical properties mostly remain identical. For example, the melting point of beeswax is around 145 to 147 degrees Fahrenheit. This melting point makes beeswax ideal for candle-making. Although you'll find candles made of different materials, the ones made from beeswax burn longer and emit a naturally pleasant aroma.

The candle from beeswax will burn slowly, produce minimum soot, and emit a bright, warm light. It's also the best option for people allergic to synthetic fragrances.

Besides candle-making, beeswax is widely used in making cosmetic products like lip balms and moisturizing lotions, to name a few. Beeswax has a natural property that allows it to stick to the skin and form a protective barrier. This keeps the skin hydrated and the moisture locked in. It is often found in lip balms, lotions, creams, and natural soaps.

Beeswax is also used in several household and industrial products. It makes the perfect soaps loaded with rich nutrients and natural materials that keep your skin clean, nourished, and full of glow. Several woodworking polishes are also made with beeswax, which enhances the natural beauty of the wood and creates a protective layer, saving it from minor scratches and environmental exposure.

Beeswax is also used in creating wax models for art, added during the manufacture of certain lubricants, and even in the food industry as a glazing agent.

Beeswax's easy handling and malleability have made it one of the most sought-after materials for art and DIY projects. It's easy to melt and mold the wax into any shape and can be used as an adhesive in woodworking. Wax paint is another popular by-product made by mixing natural pigments with beeswax and blending them while keeping the liquid's viscosity as thick as paint.

Overall, beeswax is a versatile and valuable product obtained through beekeeping. Its unique properties, including its high melting point, moisturizing capabilities, and clean burning qualities, make it a great ingredient in various industries and a popular choice for DIY projects and crafts.

The following are some other applications of beeswax.

Protective Material

Having emollient properties, beeswax is an integral material used in making quality skincare products. Its protective nature keeps the skin moisture locked, the skin hydrated, and prevents dryness. It also protects the skin from harmful environmental factors like extreme weather conditions and pollutants.

Beeswax helps to lock in moisture, keeping the skin hydrated and preventing dryness. It forms a protective barrier on the skin, shielding it from environmental factors like harsh weather conditions and pollutants.

· The non-toxic nature of this natural substance produced by bees makes it a preferred choice for those who want to use organic, chemical-free, and non-toxic products.

· The wax contains anti-inflammatory chemicals that reduce itching. Several balms use beeswax to nourish the skin when dealing with eczema and dermatitis.

· It's a natural wound-protecting substance that can be applied topically on abrasions, cuts, and burns.

· Beeswax is always harvested sustainably by experienced beekeepers, which ensures that the bee population keeps thriving and aids in maintaining biodiversity and a balanced ecosystem.

· As it's an organic material, it will break down on its own without negatively impacting the environment.

Royal Jelly

People who use royal jelly claim this natural substance can improve vitality and health and provide the body with the necessary nutrients. Worker bees produce it, primarily used to feed bee larvae and the queen. The white, creamy liquid contains proteins, amino acids, vitamins, minerals, and good fatty acids. Its nutritional profile makes it one of the most sought-after products. Some people even advocate that jelly is several times more nutritious than honey. Here are the uses and benefits of royal jelly:

Potential Health Benefits

Although scientific research is still being carried out, royal jelly has been attributed to having several health benefits. Due to the presence of essential vitamins, minerals, amino acids, and fats, the material can possibly promote the body's immune function, fight off harmful toxins present in the body, and increase the rate of metabolism. Royal jelly is also used in improving fertility, relieving menopausal symptoms, and skin health. However, more research is necessary to establish a strong basis.

Skin Care

Royal jelly is believed to contain skin moisturizing and nourishing properties, which can improve the skin's appearance and health. It's widely used in lotions, serums, and skincare creams because it is believed to keep the skin hydrated, improve smoothness, and increase elasticity.

Dietary Supplement

Royal jelly is available in several forms as a dietary supplement, including tablets, powders, liquids, and capsules. Although there's no denying that it contains essential nutrients, further research is necessary to establish its efficacy. It's recommended to take it in small doses. Doing otherwise can be pretty toxic. If you are considering using the supplement, it's best to consult your doctor first and discuss whether it would benefit you.

Precautions

Royal jelly is a naturally harvested by-product and can contain allergens. People with mild or severe allergies should always avoid using any products with royal jelly. Depending on the severity of the reaction, it can range from mild itching to flare-ups that will require immediate medical attention.

Bee Pollen

These tiny particles are collected by bees from flowering plants and trees and are used as a food source. The bees collect the bee pollen and store it in the form of small pallets. The following are the contents and uses of bee pollen.

Nutritional Content

This natural material is considered a superfood because of its rich and nutritious profile. Bee pollen contains vitamins, essential amino acids, proteins, minerals, and antioxidants. Besides containing antioxidants, bee pollen also contains enzymes required for the proper growth and development of larvae and young bees.

Antioxidant Activity

It contains several antioxidants like flavonoids and phenolic compounds, which protect the body from free radical damage. Think of antioxidants as cleaners that remove or neutralize the effect of harmful chemicals. The presence of free radicals in the body can lead to the development of chronic diseases and affect the ability of the cells to function effectively.

The flavonoids present in the bee pollen are capable of reducing inflammation. Although bee pollen has anti-inflammatory and antioxidant properties, it doesn't mean you can rely only on materials like these to address any underlying inflammatory condition or protect the body from free radical damage.

Allergy Relief

Bee pollen can be used as a practical remedy for seasonal allergies. Immunotherapy is a medical concept where controlled amounts of allergens are introduced to a person to familiarize their immune system and desensitize it. Most seasonal allergies occur due to a surge in pollen. Consuming bee pollen by yourself is never advised. Before consumption, it's best to consult a healthcare professional for the best action plan.

Performance

Consumption of bee pollen has been linked to increased physical performance. This increased athletic performance and the natural energy boost are due to the nutrient-rich composition. The amino acids in bee pollen act as building blocks for the new development of cells and repair, the vitamins boost metabolic processes, and the minerals in the pollen act as key ingredients in several performance-related body processes. In a nutshell, the collective effect of the nutrients in the bee pollen can improve performance.

Digestive Health

Some avid bee pollen users swear by bee pollen's ability to improve digestive health. They back their claim by identifying the presence of digestive enzymes, naturally present in the bee pollen, which aids in breaking down nutrients, promoting absorption, and improving metabolic activities. Still, further research is required to establish the efficacy of bee pollen related to digestive health.

Skin Health

Like other bee products, bee pollen is considered to have potential skin benefits. Its anti-inflammatory and antioxidative nature nourishes the skin, reduces swelling, and protects it from the environment.

Bee pollen can be incorporated into your diet or used for natural remedies in various ways. Start with small amounts to assess tolerance and potential allergic reactions. Sprinkle it on cereal, yogurt, or salads, or blend it into smoothies or juices. Mix it with honey or nut butter for spreads, add it to baked goods, or use it as a seasoning for savory dishes. Consult with a herbalist or naturopath for specific natural remedies. Ensure you source high-quality bee pollen and consult with a healthcare professional if you have underlying health conditions or are taking medications.

Propolis

Bees collect This resin-like material to repair and maintain their hives. Propolis is naturally antiseptic and inhibits the growth of harmful microorganisms like fungi, keeping the hive safe from infestations. Many people use propolis for its potential health benefits. It's commonly used by diabetic patients on canker sores, burns, and for oral sores. The main compounds in propolis include polyphenols and flavonoids, both antioxidants.

· The substance contains chemicals with antifungal and anti-inflammatory properties which makes the substance useful in treating skin wounds and burns.

· Cold sores and genital herpes can be treated with propolis.

· Due to its antiseptic nature, the substance can easily fight dental caries and prevent further damage to the tooth.

· Propolis is used in controlling symptoms of severe chronic diseases like multiple sclerosis, type 2 diabetes, and a few neurological disorders.

· It is being researched for its potential benefits to oral health as it has antiseptic properties to fight harmful microorganisms.

People with bee allergies should never use products containing propolis. Although reported side effects are rare, propolis can still cause skin irritation when applied topically and create mouth ulcers when ingested orally. Consuming it without consulting your doctor is never advised because the chemicals present in propolis can interact with certain medications. For example, if you take anticoagulant medication for cardiovascular health, taking propolis will increase the chances of bleeding and bruising.

Bee Venom

Another trending bee product is bee venom. It treats several chronic diseases, effectively reduces inflammation, and carries medicinal properties.

The venom is directly obtained from bees and is further processed to create tailored vaccine-like shots to treat bee sting allergies and chronic diseases like Parkinson's, osteoarthritis, nerve pain, and multiple sclerosis. Bee venom immunotherapy effectively resolves allergy symptoms in 98% of people receiving the therapy. These bee venom injections are also FDA-approved. Although there is established evidence of using bee venom shots for allergies, its use in other diseases still needs research to verify the short-term and long-term effects.

Beekeeping offers a range of products beyond honey. These include beeswax, propolis, royal jelly, pollen, bee venom, mead, and the bees themselves. Each has unique qualities and applications, offering beekeepers additional opportunities to derive value from their endeavors.

Chapter Eight

Chapter 8: Beekeeping for a Sustainable Future

Beekeeping is of great importance to the environment and the general ecosystem. It is also a source of income in rural areas, serves as a tourist attraction, plays a significant role in certain economies worldwide, and helps achieve genetic diversity in plants. A decline in bee hives and colonies would threaten all of these things. Therefore, this chapter is devoted to beekeeping for a sustainable future.

Bees pollinate, fertilize and provide wax and honey. However, the modern methods of managing and feeding bee colonies outside of their natural environment affect the future of apiculture, manipulating the process of natural selection, breeding, queen importation, and hive technology.

Apart from human influence on bee colonies, which increased greatly due to monocultures and neglect of the health of the domesticated bees and other wild bee species, global warming and climate change are just some of the environmental factors affecting the health and sustainability of bee hives. Increased temperature and weather patterns make the environment inhabitable for many organisms, including bees. Bees struggle to survive, and the likelihood of affecting biodiversity increases with each passing day.

With all of this in mind, this chapter looks at environmentally friendly beekeeping practices, pollinator-friendly habitats, their importance, and how everyone can contribute to the protection of bees and help foster a sustainable future for apiculture.

The Importance of Environmentally Friendly Beekeeping Practices

The main idea behind sustainability is making sure that the way the current generation provides for themselves doesn't affect future generations. Sustainability in apiculture refers to maintaining the balance between bee health and commercialization. Beekeeping for a sustainable future means balancing the production and commercialization of products and providing the bees with the best possible care. This practice aims to maintain and protect healthy indigenous species.

People need to engage in more environmentally friendly beekeeping practices to achieve sustainability in apiculture. With the current rise in human population and the environment's condition, these practices must be reinforced alongside new and improved techniques.

Environmentally friendly beekeeping practices include using natural methods, eliminating antibiotics and chemicals, and collecting pollen and honey in quantities that don't harm the bees. Other ecologically friendly beekeeping practices include preserving and increasing bee populations, natural intervention techniques to enable the production and survival of bee colonies, preventive measures to reduce the spread of disease in the colony, keeping nuclei alive and using them as bee and brood banks, providing clean water sources, flower-rich landscapes, plant resin, and abundant nectar.

The benefits of using environmentally friendly beekeeping practices include: conserving native and viable bee populations, increasing productivity and maintaining the welfare of bee hives and colonies, and sustaining natural ecosystems. With the increase in demand and factors plaguing the health, welfare, and life span of bees, environmentally friendly beekeeping practices must be employed in a manner that does not affect the ability of future generations to meet their own needs.

Pollinator Friendly Habitats

The term 'pollinator species' refers to animal species that pollinate plants in agricultural settings, cultivated gardens, and natural landscapes worldwide. Pollinators are relied upon for pollination, including bees, flies, moths, bats, and hummingbirds. These pollinators need proper food, water, and a favorable environment. These pollinators have coexisted with flowering plants and have formed intricate relationships with them.

A pollinator-friendly habitat is a space or area of land endowed with diverse flowering plants that provide nesting space and food for pollinators. The habitat, either natural or man-made, is a combination of cultivated flowering plants to provide food and space for the benefit of the pollinator. It may be specifically designed to accommodate a particular pollinator or can be an area that attracts all kinds. Examples include an open field and a botanical or conservation garden. Other examples are meadows, home and community gardens which serve as friendly habitats for pollinators scouring through lawns that lack essential resources they need.

Pollination is necessary for plant growth and diversity, so allowing pollinators to increase their survival and reproduction allows them to maintain and sustain plant growth and diversity. For bees, a pollinator-friendly habitat prevents death and, ultimately, extinction. Frequently changing weather patterns and temperature levels put bees at risk of drastically reducing their population. Helping them with the resources for their survival would prevent both domesticated and wild bee species from biodiversity loss.

If it's not addressed soon, the absence of pollinators can and will affect crop production. The estimated value of global crop losses caused directly by pollinator loss is 235 to 577 billion dollars. That shows how crucial they are to crop production. Losing pollinators means that most plants won't be able to produce, leading to food shortages and even worldwide famine.

It would also affect food variety, and you'll be left with mostly greens. You will also be left with fewer nutritional choices as most plants grown for medicine, food, and spices depend on pollination. Berries, apples, and melons, to mention a few, are among the foods that rely on pollination.

A pollinator-friendly habitat would mean a healthy ecosystem, increased possibility of food and genetic diversity due to pollination, and protection of bee diversity and population. These habitats preserve native species, create wild species, and ensure their survival. It also preserves the landscape.

These habitats can be artificially designed to mitigate the effects of climate and global warming on the natural habitat. It can include meadows, community parks, or botanical gardens designed to accommodate pollinators. The benefits of a pollinator-friendly habitat range from the preservation of native species, natural landscape, biodiversity, and facilitating reproduction in plants.

Advocating for the Protection of Bees for a Sustainable Future

There are various bee species worldwide, and their role in the ecosystem is critical to agriculture and the environment. They pollinate flowers and trees and maintain a healthy ecosystem needed for food production. Bees are increasingly endangered yearly, even though they maintain natural landscapes, facilitate food production, and preserve ecosystems. Climate change, rising temperature levels, and even technology affect bees.

As a result, protecting and preserving local bee colonies and biodiversity has become a topic of concern. To foster a sustainable future and continue benefiting from the economic value bees provide, you must take steps to advocate for both their safety and that of their habitat.

Steps that can be taken to maintain bee safety and biodiversity include:

- **Plant Bee Gardens**

The lack of a safe habitat where bees can build homes and find food is a huge threat to their existence. One of the easiest ways to protect bees and give them a safe habitat is to plant or acquire a bee garden. You don't need a large space to cultivate bee-friendly plants; you can establish gardens in and across window boxes and flower pots. You can even add them to vegetable gardens.

You can create a bee garden using pollen and nectar-rich flowers with various colors, shapes, sizes, and bloom times. In line with sustainable apicultural practices, it is advised to seek native or local plants, as bees have grown used to feeding on these native plants and depend on them for survival.

· Plant Trees for Bees

Many people don't know that trees provide bees with the most nectar. A blooming tree provides nectar for hundreds, sometimes thousands of bees, to feed from. For bees, these trees aren't just for nutrition but also serve as a habitat. The leaves and resin supply nesting materials for the bees, and the wood cavities are excellent shelters. Trees manage watersheds, cool air temperatures, and are great at reducing carbon. By planting trees, you can provide bees with habitat and nutrition. Planting trees in the neighborhood and joining environmental organizations to engage in afforestation go a long way in saving the environment and bee species.

· Avoid Using Chemicals for Bees

Chemicals can cause disorientation in bee colonies. The use of antibiotics and chemical sprays to control bees and curtail the spread of disease in hives can harm bees. In your bee garden, avoid applying herbicides and pesticides. Synthetic fertilizers, herbicides, and neonicotinoids can harm bees. A bee-friendly garden can thrive and should be maintained without using harmful chemicals. Planting a bee garden aims to create a friendly ecosystem where the bees can get nutritional food sources and thrive without threat. The ecosystem is expected to be sustainable and keep itself in check through beneficial populations.

If you must apply pesticides, don't apply them directly onto the soil or when the flowers bloom. You should also use targeted organic products.

· Supporting Local Beekeepers and Organizations

Another way to actively get involved in advocating for bee protection and their habitat is to support local apiaries, beekeepers, and organizations whose goal is to ensure proper welfare for bees. Provide local beekeepers with information on environmentally friendly practices to help them and the bees. Buying from them is the easiest way to support local beekeepers. You can also devote your money, time, knowledge, resources, and manpower to volunteering in local campaigns. Research and discuss new technologies and practices that they'll find helpful. Organize fundraisers to sell local produce and enlighten the community on the effects of their activities on bees.

· Participating in Community Science Projects

There are many ways to advocate for bee protection, and joining a community science project is one of them. Community science redirects regular people's interest and passion into data-driven actions supporting scientific research. A community science project allows you to learn and share important insights and knowledge that can lead to useful and relevant research outcomes. It will enable you to collaborate with naturalists in your locality and outside to share ideas and discuss important practices about beekeeping for a sustainable future.

The idea is to use your voice and the available media to increase awareness about bees while using community science projects as a platform to get the word out.

- **Safeguard Ground Nesting Bees**

Some bee species live underground; protecting them is crucial to their survival and growth. 70% of the existing 20,000 bees in the world live underground. These species build nests and habits and house their offspring during winter to emerge each spring. These ground-nesting bees require bare, well-drained, mulch-free, and protected soil to develop and access their nest in a bright and sunny environment. You can protect them by leaving a section of your garden untouched.

- **Provide a Bee Bath**

Just like any other living being, pollinators need water. Activities of foraging and collecting cause bees to be quite thirsty, and providing a water bath that they don't have to travel far for reduces their stress and allows for more time for pollination. A simple bird bath or clean water bowl can serve as a bee bath. Break pebbles and stones into the bath so they come up and rest on the water's surface.

- **Leave Stems Behind**

30% of the bee population lives in holes inside logs, hollow plant stems, or trees. These are valuable habitats for bees, and cutting them can render those bees homeless. A hollow stem isn't an ideal habitat. Still, it is a comfortable home where bees may be shielded from overwintering. Delay chopping dead stems or flower stalks until spring. This will provide 8-24-inch-high stems, which serve as a home for cavity-nesting bees.

- **Educate Younger Generations**

Tomorrow's bee stewards must learn early about their activities, importance, and uses. They also need to be taught about the repercussions of human actions on bee colonies. Guide and inspire them with activities and lessons to inform them about bees. Share information about bees from certified organizations and local platforms with the younger generation and their educators. Get them educated using free resources and expose them to the knowledge of nature and ecology.

Advocating for bees is a step forward in fostering a sustainable future for apiculture. Beginning by researching, equipping oneself with knowledge, and sharing information across age groups and societal levels would inform people about the consequences of their actions and how they can help fight against endangering bee species.

Partnering with local beekeepers and organizations increases the profits of local beekeepers, exposing them to environmentally friendly beekeeping practices and providing resources to improve local apiaries. Protecting bee colonies means a high chance to obtain more bee produce, preserve biodiversity and ecosystems and conserve beautiful landscapes.

Bees are crucial in the ecosystem and contribute significantly to agriculture and pollination. Activities of bees in agriculture foster productivity, creating diverse food crops, conserving aesthetically pleasing landscapes, and managing a thriving ecosystem. Although bees play a vital role in the ecosystem, they continue to be endangered. Human efforts to domesticate bees have increased influence over them. Humans have begun to manipulate bee colonies by managing, feeding, and transporting bees from their natural habitat to a less suitable environment for cultivation. They also focus more on their apiaries and less on the welfare of the bee colonies or the wider populations.

The reduction in bee species and population has made the subject of a sustainable future in apiculture an important discourse. The idea of apiculture for a sustainable future is to ensure the bees are in good condition, not in danger of extinction, environmental stress or chemical-induced stress, or disorientation, and can live and meet the needs of the current generation without limiting their ability to provide for the next generation.

Beekeeping for a sustainable future is geared towards balancing commercialization, production of bee products, and bee welfare.

Bees must be protected and provided with essential resources to mitigate the effects of climate change, global warming, and human activities. To achieve sustainability, environmentally friendly beekeeping practices must be employed at a large scale. Natural practices that preserve and maintain bee populations avoid the applications of pesticides, antibiotics, and synthetic chemicals to control bees, clean water sources, and bee gardens to allow bees to exist in a blooming ecosystem are all measures that should be taken seriously.

Pollinator-friendly habitats also come into play if the goal of sustainable apiculture for the future is to be achieved. Advocating for bee welfare, enrichment, and preservation of bee habitats contributes to achieving sustainability in apiculture. Beekeeping will only become sustainable if you practice more bee-friendly strategies like caring for the bee population, cutting down on honey consumption, creating friendly habitats, and spreading the idea of a sustainable future for apiculture.

Beekeeping for a sustainable future requires a holistic approach that encompasses the well-being of the bees and the preservation and creation of pollinator-friendly habitats. Beekeepers need to advocate for bee welfare, enrich their environments, and actively contribute to preserving bee habitats. By embracing bee-friendly strategies such as caring for the bee population, practicing responsible honey consumption, establishing and maintaining pollinator-friendly habitats, and spreading awareness about the importance of sustainability in apiculture, we can pave the way for a sustainable future. This sustainable approach to beekeeping benefits the bees and their vital role as pollinators and ensures the longevity and productivity of the apiculture industry. With a conscious effort and an unwavering commitment to sustainable practices, people can foster a harmonious relationship between humans and bees, preserving these creatures and their invaluable contributions to our ecosystems for generations.

Conclusion

Beekeeping is an ancient practice that has been valued for centuries. It involves nurturing and managing honeybee nests to guarantee their well-being and performance. If you're new to beekeeping, you'll quickly realize that consistent learning is fundamental to success.

One unique element of natural beekeeping is its condition as a dynamic and growing subculture within the mainstream apiary sphere. Even though non-naturalist keepers don't often rely on or even discount different hives designs or strategies, you can stay assured that there's a shift towards treatment-free beekeeping and the sustainable techniques that entail.

As "From Hive to Honey" comes to a close, it should be clear by now that this book is a thorough guide for aspiring beekeepers. From learning about the remarkable world of honeybees to managing their hives and generating delicious honey, you have explored all the knowledge and skills essential to start beekeeping.

One crucial takeaway is understanding the biology and behavior of honeybees. By recognizing their functions, behaviors, and internal operations, you can make enlightened decisions and implement the proper monitoring techniques. This guidebook also looked into hive types and highlighted their benefits and all the factors you need to consider. You have also learned about obtaining honeybees, guaranteeing their well-being, and managing possible challenges like pests, illnesses, and environmental factors.

By prioritizing all-natural and easy techniques, you can guarantee your colonies' productivity and wellness while adding to pollinators' conservation. This book also discussed integrated pest management, chemical-free strategies, and environment enhancement to support honeybees and other essential pollinators.

Pollinators play a significant role in the environment, and looking after honeybees is crucial to guarantee their survival. By becoming a beekeeper, individuals can positively impact the environment and enjoy a rewarding hobby while doing so. Besides teaching you everything you need to know, this guidebook encourages you to embark on this journey, learn from experienced beekeepers, join local associations, and stay updated to improve your skills and the colony's well-being.

People can continue to enjoy honey for generations by cultivating a future where honeybees thrive. The world needs more passionate beekeepers, and you could be one of them!

References

"3 Best Types of Beehives: Langstroth, Top Bar, and Warré | Beekeeping 101 | The Old Farmer's Almanac" https://www.almanac.com/beekeeping-101-types-of-beehives

"Beekeeping Equipment to Get Started – Bee Built" https://beebuilt.com/pages/beekeeping-equipment

"What You Need to Know About Apiary Layout - Backyard Beekeeping" https://backyardbeekeeping.iamcountryside.com/hives-equipment/apiary-layout/

10 awesome roles of bees in a hive (#2 and #5 are surprising!). (n.d.). Benefits of Honey. https://www.benefits-of-honey.com/roles-of-bees-in-a-hive/

10 ways to save the bees. (2020, September 3). The Bee Conservancy; The Honeybee Conservancy. https://thebeeconservancy.org/10-ways-to-save-the-bees/

7 top benefits of keeping bees. (n.d.). Betterbee.com. https://www.betterbee.com/instructions-and-resources/7-top-benefits-of-keeping-bees.asp

Bee hive hierarchy and activities. (n.d.). Big Island

Bees. https://bigislandbees.com/blogs/bee-blog/141373 53-bee-hive-hierarchy-and-activities

bee-health. (n.d.). Best management practices for beekeepers and growers – bee health. Extension.org. https://bee-health.extension.org/best-management-practices-for-beekeepers-and-growers/

Beekeeping safety tips. (2019, January 5). Beekeepinginsider.com; Beekeeping Insider. https://beekeepinginsider.com/beekeeping-safety-tips/

BEESWAX: Overview, uses, side effects, precautions, interactions, dosing, and reviews. (n.d.). Webmd.com. https://www.webmd.com/vitamins/ai/ingredientmono-305/beeswax

Brahmbhatt, P. (2020, June 10). How to practice sustainable beekeeping? BeehivelyGroup. https://www.beehivelygroup.com/how-to-practice-sustainable-beekeeping/

Brundell, S. (2022, February 28). 5 useful bee products (that aren't honey). New Zealand Honey Co.TM. https://newzealandhoneyco.com/blogs/honey-articles/5-useful-bee-products

Creating pollinator habitat – 5.616. (2018, January 29). Extension; Colorado State University Extension. https://extension.colostate.edu/topic-areas/insects/creating-pollinator-habitat-5-616/

Diseases: For beekeepers: ...: The Laboratory of Apiculture and Social Insects: University of Sussex. (n.d.). Susse x.ac.uk. https://www.sussex.ac.uk/lasi/resources/beekeepers/diseases

Ecocolmena. (2022, March 19). Life cycle of honey bees. Ecocolmena; ASOCIACIÓN ECOCOLMENA. https://www.ecocolmena.org/life-cycle-of-honey-bees/?lang=en

EcroTek, (2021), Harvesting Honey | A Guide For Beginner Beekeepers. https://www.ecrotek.com.au/blogs/articles/guide-for-beginner-beekeepers

Faculty By Department, & Find a Physician. (n.d.). Bee pollen. Rochester.edu. https://www.urmc.rochester.edu/encyclopedia/content.aspx?contenttypeid=19&contentid=BeePollen

Giampieri, F., Quiles, J. L., Cianciosi, D., Forbes-Hernández, T. Y., Orantes-Bermejo, F. J., Alvarez-Suarez, J. M., & Battino, M. (2022). Bee products: An emblematic example of underutilized sources of bioactive compounds. Journal of Agricultural and Food Chemistry, 70(23), 6833–6848. https://doi.org/10.1021/acs.jafc.1c05822

Grozinger, C., & Anton, K. (n.d.). Honey bee management throughout the seasons. Psu.edu. https://extension.psu.edu/honey-bee-management-throughout-the-seasons

Grozinger, C., & Anton, K. (n.d.). Honey bee management throughout the seasons. Psu.edu. https://extension.psu.edu/honey-bee-management-thr

oughout-the-seasons

Hill, A., RD, & LD. (2018, October 3). 12 potential health benefits of royal jelly. Healthline. https://www.healthline.com/nutrition/royal-jelly

HoweyFlow, (Jun 12, 2020), Is There a Best Time Of Day To Harvest Honey Using Flow? https://support.honeyflow.com/is-there-a-best-time-of-day-to-harvest-honey-using-flow/

Johnson, J. (2021, May 18). Bee pollen: Benefits, uses, side effects, and more. Medicalnewstoday.com. https://www.medicalnewstoday.com/articles/bee-pollen

Keck, M. (n.d.). Beekeeping equipment – protective clothing. Tamu.edu. https://extensionentomology.tamu.edu/files/2021/01/Beekeeping-Equipment-Protective-Clothing-ENTO-097.pdf

MarkW. (2018, November 5). The honey bee life cycle. PerfectBee. https://www.perfectbee.com/learn-about-bees/the-science-of-bees/honey-bee-life-cycle

Mites, V. (2019). Best management practices for hive health a guide for beekeepers. Honeybeehealthcoalition.org. https://honeybeehealthcoalition.org/wp-content/uploads/2019/01/HBHC_Hive_BMPs_v1.0_reduced.pdf

Safe beekeeping practices. (2021, September 13). Agriculture Victoria.

https://agriculture.vic.gov.au/livestock-and-animals/honey-bees/handling-and-management/safe-beekeeping-practices

Simmonds, M. (2022a, June 8). The importance of good beehive management practices. BeeKeepClub. https://beekeepclub.com/the-importance-of-good-beehive-management-practices/

Simmonds, M. (2022b, June 15). How to get bees to make more honey. BeeKeepClub. https://beekeepclub.com/how-to-get-bees-to-make-more-honey/

Strachan, S. (2020, October 23). Beekeeping and sustainability. Te Kapu Apiaries. https://tekapuapiaries.co.nz/blogs/news/beekeeping-and-sustainability

Sustainable beekeeping. (2022, October 18). Pacific Resources International, Inc. https://www.shoppri.com/blogs/news/sustainable-beekeeping

Tarpy, D., & Keller, J. (n.d.). Disease management and guidelines for the honey bee. Ncsu.edu. https://content.ces.ncsu.edu/disease-management-and-guidelines-for-the-honey-bee

The Colony and Its Organization. (2010, May 11). Mid-Atlantic Apiculture Research and Extension Consortium. https://canr.udel.edu/maarec/honey-bee-biology/the-colony-and-its-organization/

The history of beekeeping. (n.d.). Queen Bee Farms. https://queenbeefarms.ca/pages/the-history-of-beekeeping

The importance of pollinator habitat. (n.d.). Mariposa Gardening & Design. https://www.mariposagardening.com/blog/the-importance-of-pollinator-habitat

Thomas, E. (2021, May 19). Breakdown: Why bees are important to the environment. Action News 5. https://www.actionnews5.com/2021/05/19/breakdown-why-bees-are-important-environment/

Thompson, S. (2019, September 14). The evolution and history of beekeeping. Powerblanket. https://www.powerblanket.com/blog/the-evolution-of-beekeeping/

Underwood, R. (n.d.). A quick reference guide to honey bee parasites, pests, predators, and diseases. Psu.edu. https://extension.psu.edu/a-quick-reference-guide-to-honey-bee-parasites-pests-predators-and-diseases

Venis, S. (2021, July 30). 5 reasons why saving the bees is so critical for both people and the planet. Global Citizen. https://www.globalcitizen.org/en/content/importance-of-bees-biodiversity/

What personal protective clothing do beekeepers need? (n.d.). Betterbee.com. https://www.betterbee.com/instructions-and-resources/protective-beekeeping-gear.asp

WholeFedHomestead, (2017), How to Package, Store, and Sell Honey, plus Creative & Inexpensive Honey Labels https://wholefedhomestead.com/how-to-package-store-and-sell-honey-plus-creative-inexpensive-honey-labels/?a mp=1

WholeFedHomestead, (2017), How to Package, Store, and Sell Honey, plus Creative & Inexpensive Honey Labels https://wholefedhomestead.com/how-to-package-store-and-sell-honey-plus-creative-inexpensive-honey-labels/?amp=1

Why bees are essential to people and planet. (2019, May 20). UNEP; United Nations Environment Programme. https://www.unep.org/news-and-stories/story/why-bees-are-essential-people-and-planet

Wikifarmer, (2023), Beehive Honey Collection – Honey Extraction Basics https://wikifarmer.com/harvesting-honey/

Printed in Great Britain
by Amazon